Anorexia Exposed

BY LESLEY PANTEL

"Anorexia Exposed"
Copyright © 2021 by Lesley Pantel

All rights reserved. No part of this publication may be reproduced, digitally stored, or transmitted in any form without written permission from [the Publisher name].

All bible quotations are taken from the Holy Bible, New International version. Copyright 1984

Some names and identifying details have been changed to protect the privacy of the people involved.

Cover photo by Jason Tey @ Jason Tey Studios
Cover Design by Kellie Book Design
Typesetting by Kellie Book Design

All enquiries regarding this publication and speaking engagements:
pantellesley@gmail.com

ISBN 978-0-646-87633-7

Dedicated to:
Mum & Dad

Contents

INTRODUCTION	1
GROWING UP	3
GROWING PAINS	5
BLURRED VISION	9
THE DIAGNOSIS	11
ESCAPE TO NOWHERE	15
SURVIVAL	17
DETOUR FROM DESTRUCTION	19
TRYING TO GROW UP	23
DESPERATE FOR ANSWERS	27
DEADLY OBSESSION	29
SUPERNATURAL RESCUE	33
THANKS BUT NO THANKS	37
LOVED TO LIFE	39
THE BATTLE	41
HE LOVES ME	45
YOU ARE LESLEY	49
WHO IS LESLEY?	51
FORGIVING MY WAY TO FREEDOM	59
SPIRIT AND FLESH	61
ADDICTED TO CONTROL	65
MIND YOUR OWN BUSINESS	71
HE IS IN CONTROL	75
TAKING LIFE BACK	79
THE PRIZE	85
OUT OF THE MOUTH OF BABES	87
SUMMARY	89
JOHN'S MESSAGE	93
THANK YOU	97

Introduction

My bedroom seemed bigger than usual, and the space felt empty. I lay down on my bed, filled with dread and hopelessness. I had so much of the day left, and I had no idea how to make the hours pass away. My tummy was sore from being so hungry, and the tormenting voices in my head left me feeling emotionally drained.

"You're a hopeless case."

"Noone cares about you."

I could hear my family in the other room. Their voices and laughter only reminded me of how distant I had become from them. I was nothing more than an empty shell. Surely, they would be better off without me?

I began to cry, but this would only increase to uncontrollable wailing. I lay there, contemplating the horrible nightmare I was living.

Years of battling the destructive cycle of Anorexia had left me wishing it would all just end.

It wasn't long before my mum came in, desperate to comfort her once happy and energetic daughter. I wanted nothing to do with her attempts, and my wailing and hysteria would only get louder and more distressing.

Not long after mum left the room, the door opened again. I felt someone sit by me on the bed. Another family member's desperate attempt to reach out to the person they once knew.

I pressed my face further into the pillow and didn't want to make any contact with them. I shrugged away as they attempted to comfort me. I was inconsolable. They remained, even though my rejection was harsh and cruel. I peeked to see who was sitting alongside me. It was my dad.

I'd never really seen my gentle dad cry or show much emotion, but tears fell from his eyes as I looked up. The look on his face said it all. It was the face of a grief-stricken and desperate father. His face was almost unrecognisable. His pain and suffering were visible to see. My sense of hopelessness turned into despair and guilt.

I didn't want to be doing this to myself, and I despised the grief and pain I was causing my loving parents and my whole family.

Why was I doing what I was doing?

Are you in a space full of hopelessness and dread?

Do you feel alone and can't find a door out of the situation you find yourself. Maybe you are watching someone inside a space that you want to rescue, but it doesn't matter how loud your pleads are; nothing you say seems to be heard.

Anorexia kept me in that space for ten years.

Whether you are in that space or are watching someone struggle, or maybe you want to understand how and why someone ends up in such a hopeless space. I believe this book will benefit you and give you hope.

I want to share with you my journey through and out of Anorexia. A journey that drew me closer to God and resulted in me discovering the person He created me to be.

Three individual people prompted an unconventional recovery plan.

Sandra was one of those people. We began as friends, and soon she would help guide me through and out of Anorexia with her dietetics training and her selflessness. I will introduce her in chapter 8, and she will continue to add her insight and perspective in the chapters to follow.

Growing Up

I was born on 29th January 1974, the youngest of seven girls. We were close in age and in our relationship with one another, as expected from a large family sharing a modest home.

We always referred to the three older girls as the "three big kids" and us younger four as the "four little kids."

I was intrigued and in awe of the three big kids. They lead the way. Venturing and pushing every boundary that our parents put before us. I would spend many Friday and Saturday nights watching them get ready for a regular weekend at the local roller skating rink.

Apart from when I was very young, we didn't spend a lot of our upbringing with our extended family. Mum and dad were very private people, and many of our relatives lived overseas. My immediate family was all I really knew, and this was what was familiar and safe.

I have many great memories of time spent with my sisters, laughing and clowning around at the silliest things. We would make our own fun out the back of our home, spending the whole afternoon squirting each other with the garden hose and running through the sprinklers.

I enjoyed making people laugh. I would often dress up or do voice impersonations, and nothing would feel as good as hearing others around me, laughing hysterically. I thrived on their approval.

I probably cared too much about others' thoughts, but I enjoyed how it felt to be liked and accepted.

I was very aware of my position as the youngest member of the family. I wasn't concerned that money wasn't in abundance, but I would often consider the sacrifice mum and dad made to give us the best life possible. They never asked for anything in return, but I often felt the burden for them. I never wanted them to question their decision to have us all, mainly me, being the last of six others.

I was lucky enough to be surrounded by many kids on our street. I met Derek at the age of 6. He quickly became my best friend. It was funny, though, as we were inseparable outside of school, but while at school, we wouldn't dare be seen together! We spent most, if not every day, knocking on each other's door, gathering all the other kids in the street, and hanging out together playing.

I grew up with a belief in God. I didn't have a personal walk or relationship with God, but I had a deep understanding that there was a greater force, and I never questioned it. We would spend our early years going to church and Sunday school. I never liked being separated from my sisters, but I knew it was something I just had to do, and it was right.

In hindsight, my drive and motivation to please people were driven by fear and guilt and as the world around me got bigger, this need to please everyone would become an impossible task. I remember an evening when I reflected on the day I'd had and the conversations I'd had with my family. For no apparent reason, I began to feel an enormous amount of guilt about how I 'may' have spoken or treated any of my older sisters. Feeling uncertain of their approval, I decided to write each of them a note and apologise, just in case. Being able to confront within the family was not easy for me, so for someone like myself who was almost obsessed with others' approval, I would continuously be observing everyone's moods and body language. It was an exhausting way to live, but I was terrified of people not liking me and was convinced it was the only way to stay sure of their approval and feel some sense of control.

Growing Pains

Lyn was two years older than me, and we grew up very close to one another. Lyn was the fun sister, and she always saw the humorous side of life. She was quite different from me, and that's probably why I always loved my time spent with her. Lyn was full of adventure and didn't mind pushing the boundaries. On the other hand, I felt the need to remind Lyn of the boundaries and keep everyone in line, as I believed this would only make mum and dad's job easier?

I remember a situation we found ourselves in, where we found a packet of cigarettes. We dared each other to have a puff. I put the cigarette into my mouth back to front and tried to light it! I quickly spat it out, and it wasn't long before the guilt set in, and my choices weighed me down. I couldn't sleep the whole night. Knowing how irresponsible my decision was and how disappointed I believed mum and dad would be. I told Lyn how bad I felt and that I needed to confess to our parents what I had done. She could not believe what I was telling her and told me not to worry about it. I wished I could have been as free as she felt, but I couldn't shake off the guilt and burden I felt. I wouldn't say I liked the idea of my parent's disapproval, particularly after all they sacrificed for us.

As teenagers, Lyn and I would spend most weekends at the local roller-skating rink, repeating the footsteps of the "three big kids." It was where they spent their weekends, and it was now our turn.

I had always been interested in exercise and fitness. Any chance I had, I would put on my gym gear and dance around my bedroom to my favourite music. I had even joined the gym with one of my older sisters to keep myself fit.

My body was changing, and I was slowly evolving into a young lady from a little girl. My life and future were all before me.

I remember an afternoon when I was out driving with one of my sisters. I would have been around 13 years old. We pulled up at a shop to pick up some snacks, and I proceeded to walk inside. There was another car pulled up alongside us, with several men inside. As I walked past; they made suggestive comments and continued to stare at me as I stepped inside. I didn't feel comfortable. I was beginning to experiment with makeup and fashion, but I didn't feel any different than the little girl I was not that very long ago. I wasn't ready to be grown up, and I wasn't sure I could even pull it off.

The time in my life when I should have been experiencing and expressing my teenage years were years of fear and self-doubt.

I recall a situation I found myself in that seemed to confirm my fears of not being able to please and be liked by everyone.

I would have been around fourteen years old and had just started dating a guy who was a few years older than me. It was the first guy I had ever dated, as I struggled with having any romantic feelings when it involved the opposite sex. I believed they were bad feelings and were a sign of a lack of control and immaturity.

I had reluctantly entered into this relationship but assured myself I could handle it.

One day we were together in his bedroom at his parent's home. He began to kiss me, and within a short time, I knew his intentions were more than just kissing. There was no communication between us, but I knew where he wanted this to go, and I was terrified. I made it clear with my body language that I didn't want the same thing, and we left the room together.

It was an awkward moment, and I left for home shortly after. It's no surprise that that was the last time I would hear from him, and I was informed by a third person that he wanted to end the relationship.

Although I didn't question my decision not to follow through with his sexual advances, I was shattered. Not only because I had been dumped, but because I realised that if I did not please someone, I would ultimately be rejected. I wouldn't say I liked how this felt. I knew it would be impossible to please everyone, but this overwhelmed me.

How would I survive in this big world that only seemed to get bigger and involve more people to please? It felt like a juggling act, and every day seemed as though another ball was being added.

I had always been happy at school, but things had changed. Some of my closest friends had gone to another high school. My friendship with Derek was getting too hard to spend together. Other people continually mocked us for hanging out together. There were changes at home, a few of my sisters moved out, and my once safe and familiar place didn't feel the same. There was a sense of losing control of my once predictable and straightforward life. I felt alone.

I wasn't overweight, but I believed that if I could just lose a little weight and be more like the slim, popular girls at school, then life would be that little bit easier?

I loved food, so dieting was daunting, but I figured with not much else happening in my life, it would give me something to focus on, and the idea of being "skinny" excited me.

Walking home from school one day, I began to talk quietly to myself.

"Eating less will lead to weight loss."

"Other girls can lose weight, so you can too."

I was determined not to go straight into the kitchen pantry. I was no sooner in the house, and all I could think about was food. I was so hungry, but I wanted to avoid eating anything until it was dinnertime. If I could prevent the after-school food binge, I could lose a few unwanted kilos.

I threw my school bag down, and without another thought, this uncontrollable urge came over me. I headed straight for the pantry and fridge. I grabbed everything and anything that my eyes could see, shovelling food into my mouth until I could barely stand up. I lay on the couch, groaning in pain. All I could think about was all the food I had just consumed.

Guilt and regret hit me like a tidal wave, 'You are such a pig, and you have absolutely no discipline and should be ashamed of yourself.' I could hear these words going around and around in my head. I knew the guilt would now taunt me the rest of the evening.

If only I could have been stronger and showed some more willpower. I was disgusted with myself. I felt like a failure, a failure to myself.

I would confront this dilemma each afternoon, fighting the urge to overindulge. As each day passed, I found myself slowly making small steps toward my weight loss goal.

One afternoon as I self-talked my way home, I was determined to make this day different. Although my mind wrestled with the same thoughts, I managed to walk into the house and avoid going into the kitchen. I didn't even want a snack. I figured it was time to stop with the snacks, and I could wait for the following main meal.

My stomach was growling with hunger, but I encouraged myself that I could do it. I decided to take the dogs for a walk instead and was relieved when it was time for dinner. I was proud of what I had achieved. Now the next goal would be to decline dessert and any late-night snacks. As I crawled into bed, I was thrilled with what I had accomplished. My focus was now on repeating it the following day.

ANOREXIA EXPOSED

Blurred Vision

The days turned into weeks, and before I knew it, I had established a new, healthy routine after school. Even I was surprised by the level of discipline and self-control I was able to maintain. I continued exercising, and this became my new focus, but I just wasn't satisfied.

My weight loss had become a little noticeable, and I enjoyed the attention and compliments I was receiving. Rather than thoughts of guilt and disgust to battle, I was filled with praise and a sense of control.

"you are going to be more liked when you're skinny."

"All of your problems will seem less important."

I remember one day walking home from school, contemplating the progress I'd made. My achievements were now a way of life, but it wasn't enough. I wanted to achieve more from my weight loss.

I remember thinking how easy it had become to cut out all the snacks from my day. I wanted to achieve more. The only option I could see left was to cut out one of my main meals.

Over time, this, too, was achieved, but that same sense of dissatisfaction continued. Before I knew it, missing dinner became missing lunch, to then trying to skip breakfast. I had only one more goal, and that was to eat nothing.

Mum was beginning to become suspicious. She would notice my dinners left in the microwave from the night before and rushing out the door in the morning, declaring that I'd run out of time to have breakfast and would have something later. Not that I ever did.

The effects of not eating were beginning to take a negative toll on my body. I was becoming irritable, impatient, withdrawn, and extremely tired. I would generally come home from school, retreat to my bedroom, and sleep, often waking due to my stomach's hunger pains.

Besides all of these adverse effects, there did appear to be one positive result I was experiencing. My time had always been about the need to please others and feel their approval, but suddenly, it felt as though the tables had turned, and people were beginning to be concerned for me, and I permitted myself to be on the other side.

I liked how this felt. It was a welcoming change and a great relief to feel this pressure I had put on myself taken away. Finally, people are worried about me. I couldn't hide my lack of eating for much longer, and I felt the pressure of my mum's watchful eye.

After a lot of calorie counting and research, I decided I would introduce some breakfast. I believed this would prevent any suspicions from mum. My measurements were deliberate, and I would not consider any other option than what I had decided to have at each breakfast. I remember how angry and distraught I became when I realised the cup I had been using to measure my "milk allowance" got accidentally broken. This completely upset my rigid routine and my controlled measurements.

One evening as I sat watching tv with my dad, I was beginning to feel extremely hungry. My body was groaning with hunger pains, but I certainly didn't want to start snacking again. I contemplated having just a small snack to get me through the night when an almost audible voice resonated inside my head, 'You CAN'T eat.' The thought of the guilt I would feel made it impossible for me to contemplate eating any further. I was familiar with that accusing voice in my head, and it left me no choice, which scared me. At this point, I knew I was caught up in something more than I could physically overcome. I was no longer in control; instead, something had control of me.

The Diagnosis

It wasn't long after the incident in our lounge room that I suggested to mum that I see a Doctor. I couldn't put my finger on precisely what was wrong, but I knew something wasn't right, and I needed help.

The next day mum took me to the local doctor. He had his suspicions but made no conclusive diagnosis. He ran some general tests, and he requested me to come back in a week. By the time the week had passed and it was time for me to return to the doctor, my weight had dropped significantly. All my test results had come back clear, and I could not give him any reasonable explanation as to why my weight would have fallen.

The doctor then turned to my mum and explained what an eating disorder was. Although I was stunned at what I was hearing, it did all make sense, and I didn't try to defend the diagnosis—anorexia nervosa.

After a lengthy discussion, he would refer me to a child and adolescent clinic to see a child psychologist. A part of me was silently relieved that what I had been feeling and doing had a name. Now that there was a diagnosis, I believed we could bring it under control, and I would start to feel more like myself again.

Walking into the Psychologist's rooms for the first time was surreal. I believed I had always made responsible choices in my life, so I couldn't get my head around why I needed to seek help to make myself feel better? I felt guilty that I was having mum take me to this appointment when I knew how busy she already was. I was confident, though, I would be back to my happy self with a bit of guidance from the Psychologist. Thankfully, I was unaware of the further ten years of different doctors, psychologists, psychiatrists, and hospital admissions.

I was surprised that this one visit didn't fix my current situation, and it was apparent I needed to continue seeing the Psychologist.

No one was more surprised and frustrated than me. By the time I was fifteen years old, my situation had gone from bad to worse. My eating habits had become so controlled, and my mealtimes were a ritual of rules and regulations. I had started weighing myself daily, and staring at the numbers on the scales had become a daily obsession. I had become withdrawn from most people and disinterested in most of the things I once enjoyed.

I struggled at school to concentrate, and I felt distant from any of the friends I had left.

I decided I didn't want to continue at school any longer. I approached mum and asked her if I could leave school and look for a job. By this stage, mum and dad could see my fragility and struggle to cope with the negative changes they were observing. They would have no doubt hoped that any change could bring about a positive and improved outcome, so they agreed for me to leave school prematurely.

Fortunately, I landed a great job in a dental practice. Being the newest and youngest member of the team, I felt nurtured by my colleagues.

My work became my safe place. I could go to a place where for now, no one knew much about the Lesley I was and all my hidden secrets.

Going to work also gave me a slice of the day to be somewhat distracted from the reality of my obsessing over food. I did my best to fit in, although so many parts of my life were dysfunctional and out of balance. I would avoid eating lunch in the shared lunchroom and often find a place to sit alone.

I continued seeing the Psychologist, and although happy with my new job and position, my weight continued to drop, and the doctors weren't happy. Although my circumstances had changed for the better, I couldn't make sense of why I continued to feel so lost inside myself, and the desire and urge to control my food and weight would continue.

I had only been working for one year in my job when the Psychologist informed me that I would be admitted to the hospital in my health's best interest. As I was still considered a child, it was a decision that I had no control over. Mum and Dad listened to the experts' advice, and before I knew it, plans were being made for me to go into a psychiatric hospital.

Fortunately, my work colleagues were incredibly and surprisingly supportive. They never discussed the topic of my eating, but It was evident I was struggling. I was not only supported, but they held my job.

Mum and Dad took me to the hospital. I was unemotional and certainly didn't want to give away how terrified I was or the fact that I even cared. At this point, I didn't know who was on my side. I certainly knew mum and dad loved me, but why couldn't they fix how bad I was feeling? Did I even want them to try and fix it, or could I do it myself? I didn't want to go to the hospital, but maybe it would fix how bad I felt inside? I knew I wanted to feel better, but I certainly didn't want to gain any weight. I was confident that I could manipulate whatever situation I would be confronted with within the hospital, as I'd become good at this.

They were to drop me off, and, unbeknown to us all, that was to be the last time I was to see them or anybody else close to me unless I would meet the target weigh-ins the doctors would set before me. I still remember the awful feeling as they walked out of the room. I could see the look of helplessness on their faces. They had lost their once happy little girl but, out of desperation of getting her back, decided to do what must have gone against every parent's instinct. To leave their child when their child appeared to need them most.

The magnitude was starting to sink in. I was left in a locked psychiatric hospital ward, alone, and for something, I didn't even want to be doing to myself. I remember crying out to them as I heard their footsteps disappear down the hospital corridor, 'Don't leave me,' I cried out. 'I haven't done anything wrong,' I sobbed. Silence followed, and I found myself alone and scared in an empty room.

It wasn't long before one of the nurses came into the room. They explained a few rules and told me dinner would be served soon. They later bought a plate of prawns to my room not long after. They were not aware that I had a shellfish allergy, and my trying to convince them appeared only as a great excuse not to have to eat. It was a terrifying place to be. I was locked in a hospital room, with no credibility to back me and what felt like me against them.

Mum was later called and confirmed my allergy. It didn't make a lot of difference, as the replacement meal only sat to get cold as I moved it around the plate and contemplated how I could get out of this place.

The nurse assigned to sit with me for this meal could see my lack of enthusiasm to eat. He felt it would help if he could read off some statistics. He would tell me the mortality rate of anorexics or the result of a starved human brain. I understood that this was his attempt to make me eat, but unfortunately, this stirred up a rebellion in me, and I decided to dig my heels further.

The days rolled on, and before too long, I had worked out that I was being deprived of any visitors, messages, or gifts until I agreed to eat and gain weight. It left me feeling angry, and I could not understand why they were choosing to punish me when I had been so good at doing that myself.

I remember about five days into my stay, confined to a bed, in an empty room, alone and with nothing to do. I longed for the company, and I understood why prisoners were placed into solitary confinement. I had developed bed sores on my buttocks from not having moved for some time. I was miserable.

Suddenly, the door opened, and the cleaner had come around to maintain the room. I had never been so glad to see somebody. She was an older lady with a joyful smile on her face. It was just a relief to have someone else in the room who wasn't there to tell me off or judge me, as I had only felt up to this point. As she cleaned, she chatted gently with me. As she went to leave the room, she passed a small book for me. It was a Bible, and she suggested I read it. I didn't have anything else to do, so I began to read the small book. It didn't make a lot of sense to me, but I remember just feeling at peace as I flicked through the pages. Days were passing, and I could not see myself anywhere close to being discharged. I felt as if I'd be locked in there forever. I knew if I were to ever get out of there, I would need to outsmart them. I decided if you can't beat them, join them. With this in mind, I came up with a plan. I realised the only way to get out of there was to eat the food and gain the weight, but once I was discharged and back at home, I could lose the weight again and get back in control—which I wanted more than anything else.

DIARY ENTRY

I do feel really scared about what I have to decide when I get out of the hospital. Maybe I just need to concentrate on getting out of here first. I know I don't want to get fat. Sometimes I still see myself as fat. I think there is a much stronger part of me saying that I really do want to get better, but I'm not sure how to go about it. I know that there is something that I really fear or there is something in me that I need to overcome, but I need to find out what it is. When I think of going back to how things were, I suppose that seems like the simple solution but not the right one. I'm really confused that I'm eating this food. What will happen when I get out. Am I going to limit myself again, or am I going to eat normally? Does that mean I just cover up anything that's there? Is it really getting back into a normal eating pattern that's the problem, or is there something else? It makes me wonder what life is about. When I think about eating normally, I see myself going out more and enjoying myself, but I also picture this fat, unhappy person who is covering up their real feelings and not knowing who they are or what they really want. Sometimes I think of how things should get better. Should I just try and stay alive each day and hope that one day everything will fall into place, or do I really have to put any effort in to find out who I really am and what I really want. I know I want to be someone I am happy with, but why do I feel if something negative happens or something I don't know how to handle, that everything would just crumble. I have got to realise that everyone will go on living their own life, and there is not always going to be the same people or the same things that will either get me down or make me feel happy.

Escape to Nowhere

As I began to eat what was in front of me, I started to gain small weight increments. Before I knew it, I was getting my privileges, and by the end of the second week, I had reached the goal weight.

The morning came of what was to be my final weigh-in and then discharged. I nervously stood on the hospital scales, and, to my horror, it appeared my weight was two hundred grams down. As I knew in the real world, this would be a normal fluctuation, but every gram mattered in this scenario. The nurse was quick to confirm my greatest fear. I would not only be staying in the hospital but I would be stripped of all privileges.

I couldn't believe what I was hearing. I was full of fear and anxiety. I jumped off the scales and ran to my room, screaming that I would be going home, and there was no way they would be keeping me another day. The nurse followed behind me. She shut my bags as I stood, frantically trying to pack them. She ordered me back to my bed, but I shouted back at her to call my parents and that I wanted to go home.

It wasn't long before mum and dad had been called, and I pleaded with them to discharge me. I assured Mum that I would continue to gain weight, and I promised I would not cut out any food, pleading with her to take me home. Mum and dad eventually agreed to take me home. We were no sooner in the car to go home than when mum suggested we stop for some lunch. I told her I wasn't hungry and would get something later. Mum slammed on the brakes. Raging with anger and frustration, she turned and screamed at me, 'You are already up to your old tricks, and you promised me otherwise.' I was terrified she would turn the car around and take me back to the hospital. I had taken my freedom for granted, but I now felt I had lost it. I felt so insecure and unsure about so many things. It felt like the world was against me. I quickly opened the car door, got out, and told them to go home without me. I can't imagine what Mum and Dad must have been feeling at this point. I felt like such a failure as I dragged my feet aimlessly along the footpath. I had no plans, goals, or dreams. Life seemed tiring and hopeless. This would be only one of many unkept promises I was to make. I felt so alone.

Survival

My weekends were not my most favourite time of the week. I had started back at work after my hospital stay, which would keep most of my week busy. I was terrified of any quiet or downtime, as this would only remind me of how hungry I was. My weekends were just time that I had to try and fill between controlled and calculated meals. Meals were usually consumed inside an empty room alone. No one would dare walk in on me during this obsessive ritual.

I was assigned to another psychologist through the hospital, but my obsession with my weight and food consumed me more than the hope of any sort of recovery.

My family was now very aware of how sensitive the subject of my weight and eating was. They tiptoed around my irrational moods and learned not to challenge my eating in isolation. There were several occasions where Dad had needed to rush me to the hospital emergency department with terrible pains in my stomach. I could barely stand from the excruciating pain, and Dad would almost be carrying me into the hospital.

As I was eating so little, the acid in my stomach was beginning to eat away my stomach's lining. My stomach would often distend, and I could taste the acid in my mouth. I was convinced it was something else, but I just chose to live in denial. I sensed the doctors had seen it many times before, and I was just another statistic of a disorder that puzzled them. I would be given a plate of sandwiches to absorb the acid and sent home.

I had become so withdrawn, and when all the family came together, I would find a place where I could be alone. I would hear them talking and laughing, and this would only make me believe they didn't care and reminded me of how removed I'd become.

If they cared, they would try harder to make me well and be sad with me. I had become so self-consumed that I couldn't see outside of the tiny and miserable existence I had created. Mum and Dad would try to come in to console me, but

I would become hysterical and would scream at them to leave me alone. Deep down, I wanted them to stay and to make the horrible nightmare I was living disappear, but I knew they couldn't make it disappear, as even I couldn't make it go away.

I remember one day crying alone for an extended period in my bedroom. Mum had come in several times to console me, but she would leave after her efforts would fall on deaf ears. I felt so helpless that I screamed at her, 'I wish I was dead.' Although the thought of dying terrified me, I believed it to be the only option to end this horrible nightmare I was living in. She was now sitting with a stranger, pleading to have her life ended. Mum left the room, and I lay sobbing alone.

I could then hear Mum and Dad yelling. The tension built in the home was evident; the stress on their relationship was beginning to take its toll. I loved my parents, and they had sacrificed everything for all of their children. How could I ever forgive myself for what I was doing to them? My feelings toward them were like an unstable pendulum. I loved them and was so sorry for what I was putting them through, but on the other hand, I was so resentful they were unable to fix my predicament.

> *A poem I wrote during this time:*
> *Mum and Dad, I see your pain as I know you're feeling it too.*
> *Even though I feel alone, I know you are also going through:*
> *The battles within that I try to fight, the struggling days, and the tears at night.*
> *The days that I feel I cant go on*
> *I feel like life is passing; all those days just gone.*
> *But your suffering too, watching these days slip by*
> *wanting just for a smile, instead of hearing me cry.*
> *You see a future and how things could be*
> *trying to convince me, but I cannot see.*
> *I'm sure for you, to watch this senseless act*
> *must be so hard to just sit back.*
> *To feel so helpless, to have no control.*
> *To be told, "you don't care, just leave me alone."*
> *Thank you for patience, thank you for love,*
> *For guidance to look for support from above.*
> *I need you both to help me get through*
> *And I'm sorry I forget the pain you feel too.*

Detour from Destruction

The last number of years had been a struggle, and being eighteen- years old wasn't what I had imagined it to be.

Mum would often come to meet me for lunch at work. There wasn't a lot said between us, and I'm sure she hoped for the day when I would be the Lesley that she once knew. My soul felt empty and hollow. I had nothing to give and could make no sense of how I was feeling. After our time together, Mum slipped me a piece of paper with a name and number scribbled on it.

She told me she had spoken to a church pastor, and they had suggested that I give them a call.

I showed little emotion or acknowledgment as I snatched the piece of paper from her and grunted a reluctant, 'Thank you.' Mum was no sooner out of sight when I ran to a telephone booth to make the call. I was more desperate than I would let on.

I phoned the number and was greeted by a kindly spoken gentleman. After a short discussion with him, he invited me to come and meet him and his wife. We agreed to meet the following day after work.

The church was located in the city, and I would meet with them both in the church office.

When I arrived, I felt incredibly nervous, but I was quickly met with a warm smile and a gentle handshake. I had become so tired of explaining my past and current situation to every professional I'd met but was willing to give this a go.

To my surprise and relief, they weren't interested in my current problem but were keen just to ask me questions about who I was. I didn't feel I had a lot to tell them and felt most of me had died, and I didn't know who I was anymore. We chatted for some time before they showed me around the church and invited me to one of the church services on a Sunday. They offered to come and pick me up from my home. As I didn't have a lot else planned in my week, I decided to take them up.

Before too long, church on a Sunday was a regular outing for me, and I soon started to feel like it was where I belonged. I also agreed to be counselled by this couple once a week from their home. Around this time, Rhonda would introduce me to a General practitioner, who would advise me to start on some antidepressants. Initially, this was difficult to get my head around. I was only 18 years old and believed I shouldn't be on such medication, but I knew I needed some help and agreed to start on them.

One Sunday morning, after Rhonda dropped me home from church, she informed me that she and her husband were moving house and could not pick me up for church anymore. She suggested I call another friend of hers that could swing by and continue to pick me up.

Without hesitating, I called Glenda, and she kindly agreed to pick me up. When Glenda arrived on Sunday morning, I was surprised at how pretty, confident, and kind she was. I'm not sure what I was expecting, but she represented everything I wished I could be and reminded me of everything I wasn't. It was easy to talk to Glenda. She was a few years older than me but seemed much wiser for her years. I felt comfortable being around her.

After she dropped me home, she wrote her number on a piece of paper for me. She offered to pick me up weekly for church and suggested I call her if there was ever a time I needed to talk to someone.

I lost contact with most school friends, and I had distanced myself from my family. I had become so used to being alone. My obsession with controlling my food had created a very lonely and isolated world. Could I let anyone in?

The tension was extreme at home, and it wasn't long before I found myself alone in my bedroom, hopeless and feeling depressed. I had left Glenda's phone number on my bedside table and contemplated calling her but feared rejection. What if she was just polite when she said I could call her? What if she was out with friends, and I was just a nuisance?

I eventually plucked up the courage to call her, and to my surprise and relief, she sounded glad to hear from me.

We spoke for a short time before Glenda invited me to come around to her home. I was there before she could change her mind, and, to my surprise, she opened the door with a welcoming smile and invited me to come in.

Glenda had impeccable taste. Her home was stylish, and everything had its place. She was currently studying, so we sat down with a cup of tea as she finished off what she was doing.

She seemed genuinely pleased to see me. I felt comfortable talking with her, and it was easy to tell her what I had been going through. I had been glad that I had made the call to her, but I didn't want to overstay my welcome. I wiped the tears away and thanked her for letting me come over before leaving to go home.

The following week, I had my counselling session with Rhonda. We talked a little about my week, and I told her how I had ended up at Glenda's house over the weekend. Rhonda informed me Glenda was moving out from where she was currently renting. Glenda was looking for somewhere else to live but was wanting someone to move in with her.

Rhonda said she had thought of me as soon as Glenda had mentioned it, and Glenda was already keen on the idea.

I had never thought about leaving home. I believed I would always just be there, but I had to stop and reflect on what it was like at home. The pressure and strain that my eating disorder was putting on my parents were enormous, and I knew they were struggling to keep their heads above water. I knew it would sadden my mum to move out, but something said it was the right thing to do.

With this in mind, I said a simple yes to Rhonda, and she said she would have Glenda call me to arrange the details. I remember driving home almost in a state of shock. I was shocked that I had said yes to moving out. It felt like I was living someone else's life. Since I was little, I always had a picture of what life would look like, and moving out just didn't seem to be part of that picture.

It wasn't easy telling Mum and Dad. I knew they would be sad and feel as though they had failed me. We cried together, and I assured them that it wasn't an easy decision, but I needed to do this for me, and they also deserved to have space. It must have been hard for them to let me go, knowing I was still so unwell. I know this broke my mum's heart, but I knew deep inside that it was the decision I needed to make and be for the best. I remember going to work the next day and telling my work colleagues. I could see they were in shock, as I'm sure to them they saw a little broken girl who needed all the support she could get. I couldn't explain why I felt it was the best decision, as I couldn't make sense of it all either.

Glenda phoned me the following day, and we made plans to meet up and work out the finer details.

Before I knew it, I had Mum and Dad drive me to the apartment with my bags packed and ready to begin a new chapter.

Glenda was out for the night but left a note advising me to unpack and make myself at home. Mum and Dad waited a while and then left me to settle in. As I unpacked and hung my clothes in the wardrobe, I burst into tears. I called Mum and told her how much I loved her and how sorry I was that it had come to this.

I got off the phone, feeling guilty and asking myself, 'Why am I doing this?

Trying to Grow Up

Glenda was easy to live with, and we had our living arrangements sorted early. She was aware of my eating disorder and later shared that she also struggled with eating issues some years ago.

I tried hard to hide my strange and obsessive eating rituals with her, but I am sure she was more aware than she would let on. Glenda had become another big sister to me, and I enjoyed my time spent with her. Sometimes I felt too vulnerable living with her, and at times she would become frustrated with my behaviour and challenge me.

I never got angry or defensive because I understood how bizarre some of my behaviours, actions, and decisions were. Even I couldn't answer why I was doing what I was doing. I knew why Glenda said what she did, and she would always apologise after every confrontation we had.

Glenda would often confront my self-punishing mindset. She would often try to encourage me to buy beautiful clothes or perfume, but I had no desire to reflect any beauty, as I felt so horrible and lost inside. I remember Glenda even trying to encourage me to decorate my bedroom and add some colour, but I saw no point. My inner world was reflected in my outer world.

One year for my birthday, she bought me some pretty cushions and told me to put them on my bed. I would later purchase some pictures to match, but I found it hard to reflect happiness and beauty. My thinking was mean and controlled. I didn't feel inside that I deserved to be kind to myself, so I found it hard to reflect this on myself.

One night, as Glenda was leaving for a social event, she suggested I consider joining the church choir. She said it would be a good way to meet new friends and get out a little more. I was anxious about opening my world up as I was aware of how abnormal I lived my life and was sure that most events would revolve around food.

It wasn't an easy decision, but I decided to join the choir, which would become part of my weekly routine.

I had begun to see a psychologist (Pip) weekly, but again it wasn't long before she was another specialist scratching their head and wondering what more they could do for me. Fortunately, she wasn't prepared to just let me go, as she knew the years of rejection I had experienced before seeing her and didn't want to leave me feeling helpless and hopeless.

The only other option she could see at this stage was to have me hospitalised. I was terrified and straight away said I would never go back into the hospital system. She calmed me down and began to explain a different approach she had been contemplating. She said that I would be admitted voluntarily, and she would set it up with a dietician. She assured me that it wouldn't be based on the typical privilege system. Instead, I would have a team of people who would work with me, and she would visit me daily.

Although I had become comfortable with my lifestyle and my work and church routine, I knew this wasn't my best life. Although I couldn't see how a stay in the hospital could help me, I was desperate. I quietly hoped that maybe something could be unlocked, and I could finally step into recovery and make my way to freedom. I was prepared to give it a go.

My work colleagues and employers were once again supportive, and this would be the first time in almost six years of working with them that I would confess to having a problem with eating. I think they were glad to hear me admit to my struggle but also relieved to hear that I agreed to help myself.

My time spent in the hospital was different this time to the last. I spent a lot of time reading and listening to my music. I was allowed visitors, and this is what I looked forward to the most. My meals were discussed and agreed upon, so I never felt losing control and was given cooking and nutrition lessons. In theory, I couldn't have asked for any more. Even the nurses were friendly and would later invite me to their homes and offer me encouragement and support.

It was certainly an eye-opening experience as I met and spoke to people from all walks of life. Everyone had a story to tell, and ultimately, we were all in there for much of the same reason—lost souls. People were searching for purpose and answers. I was making progress and small steps in many areas, but what I was aware of the most was that horrible feeling that I just couldn't explain.

One day Glenda and her boyfriend, Tony, had come in to visit me. I began to explain to them the nightmare I had the night before.

I was lying in a coffin with the lid off, terrified and filled with fear. Suddenly, an image appeared over me; it was ugly, loud, and aggressive. Death was in its eyes. I was desperate for someone to help, but the image started to mock me and hold me down. His voice was chilling me to my bones, 'I've got you. I've got you.'

My eyes opened, and I lay frozen in my hospital bed. I couldn't move.

After telling this to Glenda and Tony, they suggested that they pray for me, which they did. I never had that dream again. Tony would later bring in an audible Bible teaching, which I would listen to each night as I went to sleep.

Two weeks had passed, and my physical progress had not gone any further. Pip came to see me and asked how I was feeling. We agreed my time spent had been beneficial but decided there was probably no point in me staying any longer. She agreed to keep seeing me as an outpatient once I was discharged.

Part of me was relieved that I had stayed in control and gained no weight, but another part of me was disappointed that I couldn't walk out a new and different person.

Life went back to normal once I left the hospital. I knew others were disappointed with the little change they could see, no more than myself.

I felt like I was a hopeless case. What was wrong with me? Why was I still driven to live this life that left me isolated and depressed? I couldn't let go, and I wouldn't. A life without Anorexia still appeared unsafe.

After four years of living with Glenda, the safe and comfortable place under her mentoring, and friendship was to end.

Glenda and Tony were planning to marry, and I would need to find somewhere new to now call home. I was devastated. I was happy for her, but all I could think about was not having her around as I had for the past four years. I had no idea where I could move to. I didn't feel that moving back home was an option, as Mum and Dad were trying to make their life somewhat normal amongst all my abnormal, and I thought it wasn't fair on them.

One of the girls I was working with suggested a friend she knew was looking for a roommate. I phoned the contact number, and within the same month, I was packing my bags and reluctantly moving into a new chapter.

I wasn't excited, and I found the first few months extremely hard. I missed Glenda terribly. I felt I was only renting a room with no friendship. I felt as though I had lost the one good thing that I had in my life.

I made the best of the situation but would cry my heart out to Pip (Psychologist) at each visit, but this too was about to change.

On one of my visits to Pip, she explained that her husband had been transferred overseas and would be packing up and relocating. I didn't think things could get any worse. I was devastated. She assured me that she wouldn't just leave me. She explained to me she had already been researching some names of other therapists. She even said she would come with me to the first appointment. I burst into tears.

I didn't want to see anyone else. I loved talking to Pip, and I dreaded the thought of starting therapy with someone new again. I was so tired of re-hashing the same information to another person. I would be adding another person to my list of "failed recovery attempts." I despised the destructive cycle. Why couldn't I just stop? Why couldn't I just snap out of the mess I found myself in?

I finally agreed to take Pip's offer up, and the following week we visited my new therapist's rooms together. He greeted us warmly and put his hand out to shake mine, 'I'm Bruce,' he said. I shook his hand limply but made no eye contact.

The three of us sat down together, and Pip began to explain the situation to Bruce. His approach was professional but casual. I liked that, and after a time of talking together, he agreed to take me on and promised Pip he would do all he could to help me.

I returned to the house I was living at and sat on my bed, crying. I missed Glenda, and now I would be losing Pip. I remember looking down at my legs hanging over the bed, and the house had a flea infestation. I could see and feel the fleas jumping onto my ankles and legs. Twenty-two years old, and I still resented the place I was in. At this point, I wondered if life was worth living?

Desperate for Answers

I agreed to meet with Bruce once a week. On one of my first visits, Bruce referred to Anorexia as an addiction. I was offended, as I did not consider myself an addict. No one had ever referred to Anorexia as an addiction. I resented what I viewed as Bruce's lack of understanding and judgment.

Our weekly sessions would continue for a couple of years. We made a lot of emotional progress at that time, but my weight continued to go down gradually. I carried around with me a sense of hopelessness as every year went by, and I found myself in the same place. Bruce would never indicate any thought of him giving up on me. He continued to speak to me each week with hope, even though I couldn't see any. I also decided that I would move out of where I was living and purchase my own place. I intended to have someone move in with me, but after moving in and setting up home, I decided I was happy to be on my own. A decision that would set me up to plummet even closer to death.

It was around this time that I met Sandra.

A church woman's group met once a week and invited me to attend. I was reluctant to go, but as I rarely had any contact with anyone outside of work, I decided to go.

I had overheard Sandra talking to someone within the group. She had mentioned that she was a dietician, and this got my attention.

Sandra was easy to talk to, and I quietly hoped that she might have some answers for me within her scope of work.

She was kind, and she genuinely wanted to help me. Initially, It was more of a mentoring relationship. Sandra would give of her time so generously and would encourage me the best way she could.

From Sandra: *The miraculous thing about our meeting was that I didn't even attend the same church Lesley went to, and I only went* to one of those young woman's meetings. Lesley also didn't use to socialise and get out much, and that meeting she attended where we met was the only one that she had ever attended. She told me later that she didn't like going out and had pushed herself to go to this one event.

We often marveled about how we met, seemingly by chance but likely orchestrated by a loving God arranging help. These initial meetings with Lesley were a journey of discovery for me and perhaps a more in-depth look at Lesley's situation. I only talked very little to her about the nutritional implications of being so underweight. Firstly because she had likely heard it before, but also because it probably wouldn't change anything as it wasn't the real issue. This wasn't just a fad diet or poor eating choices to stay slim that dietary education would be able to talk her out of.

As such, I had no idea really why she would be choosing to be so self-destructive. I had learned the basics at university about Anorexia and the likely broad causes; however, what was Lesley's specific reasons? That is why dietitians will always work with psychologists to treat this condition.

Our chats were lovely but also somewhat draining on an emotional level at times for me. Lesley was depressed, and I was trying to lift her up. Depression is normal for anyone grossly underweight or with an eating disorder. The lack of nutrients in the diet affects the brain function and, therefore, mood.

Deadly Obsession

Although I continued working full time and attending church, I would be desperate to get within my home's four walls and be alone. My perception of reality became even more distorted, and I became even more isolated.

Mum and Dad were becoming more and more concerned with my erratic behaviour and grave appearance. My moods had become darker, and I was simply a shell of any former self. I would still visit their home every weekend, lost and broken. The little girl inside just wanted them to fix everything.

My visits would turn into screaming matches, and I would often retreat to one of their bedrooms, sobbing and pleading for my life to end. I saw little of my sisters as I had pushed most of them away, and they were also affected by my appearance and moods. It was a frightening and lonely time. I hated what I was doing and the life I just existed in. Ironically, I was too scared of a life without Anorexia. Taking the Anorexia away only represented me being in a vulnerable world I would have no control over. I felt I was in a no-win situation. I could see no way out of this horrible and self-destructive life I had created, and to make it worse, I felt no-one understood.

Flicking through a magazine one afternoon, I came across an article about twin sisters currently suffering from Anorexia. I latched on to their story and began to read their goal to reach a potentially deadly weight. Unfortunately, one of the twins had lost her battle, and the other was now in a black hole with no idea of how to dig herself out.

Although I empathised and connected with that demonic drive to achieve this unrealistic weight, I was challenged to see if I, too, could reach the same weight? I did not think for a minute that I could die. The challenge would override all reasoning. I was driven by that feeling of control and believed this would ease the pain I felt inside. Maybe if I could achieve this goal, it would make everything feel better again.

With this in mind, I drove straight to the shops to purchase a new set of scales to start on this deadly path.

As I watched the numbers on the scales go down each week, the voices in my head praised my efforts.

"You have such great willpower."

"Life will be so much better when you're skinnier."

I could see nothing dangerous at all in what I was doing. I focused on my recent challenge as a necessity to block out everyday life's ups and downs. I could escape those realities and venture into a world where only I could go and feel complete control. My physical appearance would only worsen, and everyone around me observed the changes, but I was oblivious.

I remember walking through the shopping centre one day, and as a mum and her teenage daughter approached me. I could hear their gasps. They continued to stare at my skeletal body from top to toe. The look of pity and shock was evident on both their faces. I didn't flinch at their response. I told myself that one day they would only see someone skinnier than me.

My family was helpless, and Mum and Dad's pleads with me would fall on deaf ears. I was so close to death that mum and dad were advised to have my affairs in order.

Even then, I refused to see what the fuss was about.

I walked around like a ghostly skeleton, but I still managed to push myself to go to work and hold down a full-time job even in this extreme state. I can't imagine what it must have been like for my work colleagues to watch me self-destruct before their very eyes. I knew they were concerned, and at times my colleagues would try and bring up the subject, but I would never enter a conversation. My workplace was where I could immerse myself into being busy and doing something I loved to do and pretending for 8 hours a day that I was as normal as everyone else. They did not want to risk saying anything that could upset me.

One morning as I lay in bed, I stared up at the ceiling and contemplated if it was even worth getting out of bed. I had lost motivation for living and figured no one would miss me anyway. I believed I'd become a burden and worry to everyone around me. The phone rang, but I was too tired to get out of bed to answer it. I rolled over and went back to sleep. The phone continued to ring, but I chose to ignore it. Eventually, I got sick of the broken sleep, and the next time it rang, I decided to answer it.

I heard Bruce's voice; he sounded shaken but relieved. I asked him what was wrong? He explained that Mum and Dad had been trying to call me all morning, but as they were unable to get hold of me, they contemplated the worst had happened to me. I didn't understand what all the fuss was about. 'I'm okay," I said and explained that I had just decided to stay in bed a little longer. I had gotten to a place where I was numb to anyone else's feelings and concerns but my own. I believed I was at the end of a bad deal, and the only person I thought about was myself.

Bruce was getting more and more concerned with my decline and, although he had promised both Pip and myself that he wouldn't give up on me, he was running out of options and ideas. On my next visit, Bruce would share his concerns with me and told me he was getting pressure from medical professionals to admit me to a hospital.

I blankly refused and, through tears, told him that it never worked and won't ever work. I knew Bruce was under all sorts of pressure, but there was no way I would agree to go back into the hospital. He sent me away and told me to think about it and get back to him the following day with my decision?

> **From Sandra:** *I noticed over this year that although with prayer, I was able to encourage Lesley at times, I was getting more distressed about her health. We were talking more often, which I didn't mind at all, but there was a sense of heaviness about the lack of progress, despite Lesley receiving good GP care and psychological counseling at the time. As she was so sad, and we were good friends by now, it affected me deeply. I also started to feel stressed and worried. I remember worrying about her and often crying over the situation as the stress of it took its toll. I felt a burden to help her through Anorexia but found that my added efforts alone were not enough. My stress levels increased as her weight crept dangerously low. I figured that two things were required. One was that Lesley needed a new recovery approach to add to what we had all done over the years, and I needed help myself to help Lesley as I was going emotionally downhill fast. I didn't want to stop helping her for one second, but I needed some support for me, and we needed a new way to tackle the weight gain recovery process. We both needed help.*
>
> *One morning during this time, I felt overwhelmed and prayed to God that I was totally at the end of my strength. I couldn't go on anymore as things were. I needed help straight away. Efforts alone were not enough.*

ANOREXIA EXPOSED

Supernatural Rescue

I had arranged to visit a Christian counsellor the morning after my meeting with Bruce. I was desperate and unsure about what my next step would be. A friend had told me about this lady who offered prayer support, so I decided I would go along to see her.

We talked for a while, and then she prayed for me. Before I was to leave, she asked me another question, 'Why do you refer to the anorexia as you?'

I wasn't sure what she meant.

She then said to me, 'Do you not ever see it as this horrible monster that you choose to carry around with you?'

I couldn't answer her, as to be honest I didn't understand what she meant. Of course, I would refer to it as me; I am an anorexic. I couldn't separate the two.

I got back in my car and headed to work. I was no clearer on my decision, and I had an appointment to see Bruce after work. The inevitable decision I needed to make was evident. I would probably need to agree to be admitted again into a hospital, or Bruce would be left with no choice but to release me from his care.

I was overwhelmed with fear, and I began to cry. I had no idea what to do, so I started pleading with God to take me. I had reached my end, and there was no way I would go back to the hospital. It just hadn't worked for me in the past, and I didn't want to try it again. I was tired of my attempts at recovery. I could only ever reflect on any past efforts to be likened to a pruning. I would make a little step forward, but after some time end up back in the same hopeless place. I wanted to be completely free, roots and all, but I could not see this ever happening. It appeared impossible.

I cried out to God again, but this time I begged him for his help. I began pleading with him to show me what to do and make it clear, as I couldn't do this on my own. Soon, I pulled into my workplace. I wiped the tears from my eyes, took a deep breath, and headed inside.

Surprisingly, I walked in to see my boss's wife waiting for me. She asked me to come to one of the offices, together with my boss. They began to share their concerns about my declining condition. They said they were worried about my general health and my ability to continue my job effectively. I felt defensive and tried to tell them that I was looking into doing something that would assist my recovery. They offered me to come and live with them while I recovered, but I just didn't feel this is what I wanted to do.

I knew that I could risk losing my job by refusing, but I was willing to take that risk. I felt trapped and knew I needed to make a decision, but I was terrified.

I was then informed I had a phone call.

I was surprised to hear Bruce on the other end of the line. He began to explain to me that he had received a phone call from Sascha, one of the members of the same church I was attending. She had asked him for some desperate advice for a "girl" suffering from Anorexia.

Bruce was advertised as not only a clinical psychologist but also an eating disorder specialist. Sascha had no idea I was seeing Bruce but decided she would give him a call as she had been watching my decline from a distance in the church, but had felt an urge to step in and come up with a plan that could offer me some hope of recovery before it was too late.

Bruce began to tell me that as soon as Sascha started to explain the situation to him, he knew it was me she was referring to.

He then asked for my first name, and of course, she confirmed they were talking about the same person, me!

As Bruce was desperate to help me, he was keen to hear what this girl, Sascha was proposing.

Bruce began to explain the idea to me. I was hearing him speak, but I wasn't listening to everything that he was saying. I could only think back to my time earlier in the car, where I cried out to God for an answer and for Him to make it clear for me what to do. Bruce mentioned that Sascha had also been in contact with Sandra, the dietician I had been catching up with over the last year. Sascha had spoken to Sandra about helping me, and Sandra was more than happy to come on board and offer any assistance and support.

I knew at this time; my desperate prayer earlier that day had been answered. I wasn't sure if I was keen on the idea of it all, but I knew I was being forced into a corner, and the only other option I had, was death. Regardless of how I felt, I found myself agreeing to her suggestion of a recovery plan.

> **From Sandra:** *Lesley rang me later this day and told me what had happened. I was amazed and knew God had answered my prayer. Relief swept over me. I was sure we had the answer to her recovery now. I knew in my heart that she would not die but live and thrive.*

I was so surprised and relieved that help was coming.

God was so good to rescue Lesley and me on a practical level. I didn't tell Lesley at the time that I had come to the end of my strength. God caught me by His hand right on the very day I thought I couldn't go on, and saved me. I was revived and could now go on and continue as support to Lesley.

This bible verse tells us why God helped us.

Psalm 91:14-16

Because He loves me, says the Lord, I will rescue him: I will protect him, for he acknowledges my name. He will call on me, and I will answer him. I will be with him in trouble. I will deliver him and honor him. With long life, I will satisfy him and show him my salvation.

We were both stunned at the turn of events. Lesley, a little alarmed at what was brewing, and me ecstatic that there seemed a way to ensure that Lesley would eat what I recommended provided we could raise a large number of volunteers. Hope had entered our hearts. I was in awe of God and His goodness.

Sascha worked hard, asking at both our church and other churches for volunteers to help in a recovery program for Lesley. She managed to get 35-40 kind people willing to help. We had several conversations to discuss what was needed in the program and how we might achieve progress. Sascha was perfect for the role as she was fully committed to Lesley, was a great organiser, bold and good at showing "tough love," and her support gave me strength.

Thanks but No Thanks

June 1998. One by one, people began to enter and fill the auditorium of the church. I sat up the front, too scared to look around at the faces sitting behind me. I had Bruce, Sascha, and Sandra seated on either side of me. Their reaction to the people arriving was very different from mine. They smiled and greeted each person that sat down.

Bruce had arranged tonight's meeting, and I was feeling anxious about this program's details, I had somehow agreed to.

Bruce stood up to speak and thanked all the volunteers for turning up and giving up their evening to attend. He continued to explain that Sandra had written up a very well-thought-out eating plan, and Sascha would roster volunteers on to sit with me at each meal, three times a day, seven days a week. Bruce would continue to counsel me every week and would oversee the whole program.

A contract had been written up and signed by the four of us. We had set a target weight, and this was agreed on. I was to be weighed each day at the same time by the breakfast volunteers, and it would then be recorded. Each set of volunteers would sit with me as I ate and record any general information and feedback.

This was a huge risk and gamble, particularly for Bruce. His professional boundaries were being stretched, but he promised to do all he possibly could and was standing by his word.

Questions were being asked by people I didn't even know. I sat and listened to my whole life, being exposed and pulled into pieces. I believed I was the victim here, and I still viewed their attempts to make me gain weight as a way of taking something valuable away from me. I believed they only wanted to take the control away from me, and then I would be out of control again. I was angry. Angry that I was even in this position, angry that I couldn't just snap out of this and live a free and independent life. I resented being there.

It was also humiliating. I didn't know what to feel, but I just wanted the night to be over.

After Bruce finished addressing the crowd, he turned to me and asked if I had anything, I wanted to say.

I remember standing to my feet, unable to look anyone in the eye, and said, 'Thanks, but no thanks.' My response was selfish and self-centred, but I didn't care.

I wanted so much to be healthy and normal. I had no idea what that looked like, but I somehow knew this was my last chance of recovery.

Anorexia was my success and achievement but seemed to conflict with my agreeing to this recovery attempt. The battle to fight this and recover, living a life free of Anorexia, was not something I could even imagine or even say I wanted. Although scared and feeling vulnerable, I just couldn't keep living the existence I now lived in.

I was prepared just to see what I would feel like and how things would look, but it was probably all I was willing to give? When the meeting came to a close, I still had people I'd never met or seen before come over even after my rude attitude. Their faces beamed as they introduced themselves and shared how excited they were to be part of something so incredible and look forward to getting to know me more. I didn't share their enthusiasm. I believed these were my last days of freedom.

> **From Sandra:** *The purpose of the volunteers sitting with Lesley was for multiple reasons. Firstly these people were a healthy and loving distraction for Lesley as she was attempting to do difficult things like eating new foods. Secondly, they would typically eat their meal with her so that she could eat with people(rather than them just watching her) and that she could even see what typical meals looked like. The volunteers were like the "police" that could check Lesley was eating what was listed for her to eat. Even though Lesley didn't have Bulimia (purging), the volunteers were asked to stay with her for at least half an hour after the meal to make sure she wasn't tempted to start this up when under new pressure.*

Loved to Life

I heard the sound of footsteps toward my front door. The first volunteers had arrived for the very first shift for breakfast.

As I opened the door, two bright faces stood before me. Welcoming them into my home went against everything anorexia had become to me: a world of secrets, rituals, self-punishment, isolation, and deprivation. As far as I was concerned, and, through years of strict willpower, I had succeeded in finding a place where I believed I was in control. I felt that anorexia was my friend that protected me from a world I wanted nothing to do with. A world where I would be hurt and where people would take advantage of me. No one was going to take this from me.

Before the volunteers arrived, I had already swapped some of the products to eat for diet brands and ones I felt comfortable with. Although Sandra had been gracious with the diet plan, I still felt very strongly the need to control what I would eat. I was not ready to trust anyone completely. I was convinced that the diet plan would drastically increase my weight and spiral out of control.

Before sitting down, I had agreed to a daily weigh-in. The battle raged in my head as I stripped down to nothing more than my underwear to expose my skeletal frame. My weight was my trophy, and I knew what the intention was. To take it from me. It didn't make sense. Why was I letting them in? Why was I revealing my secrets to them? I took a deep breath and stepped on the scales. My lowest weight was recorded.

We sat down for breakfast together, and because I had swapped the food, I appeared happy enough to eat what was in front of me. Both volunteers left after half an hour after I had eaten, and I went about my usual day of going to work until the next two volunteers would meet me for lunch. Dinner was much harder for me as Sandra introduced many new foods I hadn't eaten in ten years. If there were going to be any tears and tantrums, it would be at dinner time.

A few days passed, and so far, all seemed to be going to plan, as far as I was concerned. Sandra, Sascha, and Bruce were not as happy.

My weight had somehow dropped, and this left Sandra scratching her head.

Although they were well aware that the weight was only part of the bigger problem, they were also fighting against time. I was physically on a razor's edge between life and death. More pressure was being placed on Bruce to have me admitted into a hospital. Sandra had carefully and thoughtfully prepared my diet plan, so she couldn't understand how my weight could go down.

I knew precisely why the weight wasn't increasing and was happy to keep it this way.

> **From Sandra:** *It was when the program started that I began to use my dietic training for Lesley. I wrote up a meal plan for Lesley with graduated increases in food and calorie intake. We also discussed various weight gain strategies. So, we were nearly set to go ahead.*
>
> *At the initial meeting to set up the program, her psychologist instructed all of us to say kindly to Lesley if she didn't eat the recommended food, we were disappointed in her. Nothing else was to be said. No coaxing or reasoning was to be applied. I felt this was going to be powerful. Nobody likes to disappoint people who care for you.*
>
> *So the program started, and despite some setbacks, the wheels were in motion. I didn't set high weight goals for Lesley, as I felt this would cause undue stress. I felt that baby steps would still get us there in the end.*
>
> *I had an unexplained peace and assurance all along that she would live.*
>
> *Any measures had to be put in place to ensure the weight would increase despite Lesley's efforts to fight this. Those with anorexia want to eat in private to keep their secrets, so this certainly would have increased her stress levels.*

The Battle

Sandra spoke to me about her concerns about why my weight wasn't increasing, but I was quick to deny knowing why.

Anorexia permitted me to be deceitful and see nothing wrong with lying. However, I believed everyone was only out to gain control for their benefit, so I justified my lies.

Sascha called me the next day at work and asked if I could meet both her and Sandra during my lunch break. I headed down, anxious as to what they were going to say. I wasn't prepared to confess to my swapping of food, so it left me wondering what they would decide to do. I had already decided to stop swapping the food brands and follow what had initially been written for me. Sandra expressed her concerns about my weight decline and requested I introduce some liquid meal replacement drinks into the current diet plan. I was now feeling overwhelmed. I wasn't prepared to now confess what I had done, so if they were going to add more food, I would have to continue swapping food; otherwise, I believed my weight would balloon.

I was annoyed with myself for allowing the situation to get to this, and I resented being in this position. I could have just confessed what I'd been doing to Sandra, but I risked losing her trust so early in the program and didn't want her to be angry with me. Sandra had become such an incredibly selfless support and friend to me. She was investing countless hours encouraging and mentoring me. I couldn't let her down at such an early stage of the program.

I began to sob as I pleaded with her to give me another chance, but it was too late. Sascha and Sandra had already decided to add more food. They knew it was the difference between life and death, and time was against us.

As well as the new addition, Sascha would then advise me that if there was no weight gain after a few days, the volunteers would cease.

Although it would seem that I would be happy to have the volunteers removed, I had realised that this was my last chance. Nothing else had worked, and I knew

I didn't stand a chance attempting recovery alone. There was an internal battle going on. The voice in my head was screaming at me from both sides.

"get rid of those volunteers, and you will be back in control."

but another voice was whispering,

"These people are here to help you and your last hope."

I agreed to add in the extra drinks, but my brain was in overdrive as I tried to work out how I could work around it.

After a week of the revised eating plan, my weight would increase slightly. It was relief and joy for many, except me. I believed I was losing all control, and the voices in my head would always tell me I was being weak and letting others win.

I called Sandra and confessed to her what was going on in my head and how I felt. She listened to me and would remind me that I needed to remember that it wasn't my decision to increase my weight but hers. Somehow her owning that decision made me feel a little better, and I would remind myself of this whenever the voices came. It was a reinforced thought that was just enough for me to hang onto and keep going.

It was made clear to all the volunteers that their role was not to counsel me. Prayer was optional, and if I chose to pray before a meal, it was my decision. I knew that I would need all the help and intervention I could get, so I allowed each volunteer to pray before eating.

Although the initial weight gain was minimal, it was a huge step for all involved. I was now left focusing on the week before me and knew the intention was another slight weight increase. I wasn't ready to gain any more weight, but I was also aware of Sascha's threat temporarily stopping the volunteers. I was anxious and overwhelmed with the position I found myself in.

It was all that consumed my mind. Food and weight. I was terrified of losing control. Finally, I concluded that the only way I could outsmart them was to cheat. I decided I would fill my underwear with little pebbles. Believing this would be the only way to get my weight over the line on paper but would allow me to avoid any actual weight gain.

The morning came for the weigh-in. As I stood up onto the scales, I could feel my heartbeat racing. The volunteer stood in front of me, encouraging me every step of the way. The scales read precisely what was expected. I felt a tremendous sense of relief. As I stepped off the scales, the volunteer hugged me tightly and expressed how proud she was. Her face beamed with excitement. We sat down for breakfast, and she continued to praise me.

Once the volunteer left, I continued with my day. It was a welcoming sense of relief, and I was pleased with staying in control.

I ended the day like every other. I would say goodbye to the last volunteers around 7 pm and begin to get myself ready for bed. I hadn't been alone for long when I started to feel overly aware of my decision earlier in the day to cheat. I tried to shake it off, but I couldn't seem to get it out of my mind. Somehow I was feeling different. I couldn't quite put my finger on what it was, but I couldn't shake it off. I began to feel convicted over what I had done earlier in the day.

The volunteer had shown such excitement and encouragement when she believed I had gained the necessary weight. She was genuinely happy for me and appeared to be wanting something good for me. Yet, I couldn't shake the thought of her sacrificing her time to come and sit with me day after day.

I was not used to feeling bad for lying or cheating when it came to my eating, food, or weight. I thought I was "protecting" anorexia? I believed it to be my right.

I had no choice but to call the volunteer and tell her what I had done. She was very gracious and thanked me for being honest with her.

> **From Sandra:** *Lesley had been under the deception that she could one day achieve or reach a level of weight or eating volume that would satisfy her.*
>
> *She didn't understand that with anorexia, the goalposts keep moving.*
>
> *No sooner than you achieved one reduction in food or weight that another would pop up, just a little out of reach. The lie that she believed was that if she kept pushing on that, she would reach a level that she is happy with. Sadly with anorexia, it's never good enough. There is no satisfaction with having achieved the ultimate goal because it continually moves. It is like trying to grasp oil in your hand, impossible! Therefore what is the point of all the striving?*
>
> *Lesley was eating a nutritious but lower energy (calorie) density meal plan; therefore, the food volume would be higher than an energy-dense plan to achieve her calorie requirements. This was another reason why I encouraged her not to compare meal sizes to other people.*
>
> *Probably one of the most frequently repeated encouragements for Lesley was the one where I talked about the truth of the road she was on. She understandably disliked the road's difficulty and pain to recovery, with all its new challenges and fears. However, I would remind Lesley that staying in anorexia was also painful and challenging. The big difference between these two struggles was that the road to recovery was one where there was a chance of wholeness and freedom. Both ways certainly involved difficulty and pain, but one had gain at its end, the other only ongoing pain. Staying in anorexia might feel slightly safer due to familiarity; however, it does not lead anywhere good. Only the healing path had hope with it.*

The bible goes on to say, "therefore choose life"...and this is what Lesley did.

Equally important was the encouragement for Lesley to read her bible and attend bible studies to grow her faith.

He Loves Me

The first few weeks of the program were hard, and every day bought with it a new challenge. I continued to swap food and do all I needed to gain only enough weight to get me across the line.

I was determined to stay in control, as I was terrified of gaining too much weight and losing control.

Day after day, the volunteers continued to turn up. I tried hard to stick to the program, but some days were too much for me to cope with, and I would spend each meal time crying and unwilling to eat what was in front of me. I felt like I was living someone else's life. I'd question how I had ended up in this position and days when I would want to protect the anorexia and could only see the attempts of everyone around me as an intrusion.

I would ask myself daily, 'Why do I do what I do?' Nothing made sense and I could only guess how long the volunteers would hang around for before they too would give up on any hope of recovery for me.

I would be keen to have some quiet time alone by the end of each day. Once the last volunteers would leave after the evening meal, I would often crawl into bed and write in my diary. Putting pen to paper would help me express my worries and fears. I wasn't good at praying out loud, but I often found myself addressing it to God, when I wrote. I wasn't sure if he was ever listening, but somehow it made me feel better.

I had always been aware of God, but I would often hear people referring to Him as though they knew him personally. This was not how I knew God. I had made it my goal in life to have and be in what I believed to be complete control, so I had never made any room for God to be any more than a spiritual being I would hear and sing about at church on a Sunday.

In August 1999, I wrote in my diary and told God how hard the day had been and how I feared to continue with the program. I felt it was only a matter of time before I would disappoint everyone helping me, and I was only wasting their time. I was desperate. I hated what I was doing but somehow couldn't let go.

I paused for a moment before closing my diary when I heard an almost audible voice, 'I love you.'

Not only did I hear those words, but I felt them. It was as though someone was standing next to me, speaking those words straight to me. I asked the question out loud, 'Jesus loves me?'

I heard it again, 'I love you.'

Suddenly, a sense of warmth and safety filled my room, a peace I had never experienced before. I began to cry as I questioned again whether those words were meant for me? There was no denying that these words were intended for me to hear and know that God loved ME.

At that moment, with those three words spoken, I knew that he loved me, and for the first time, I heard his voice as a Father. He had created me. His precious child.

Anorexia, and all it was, reflected someone unworthy of any love, not worthy of joy because of all my imperfections.

I fell to my knees and began to cry out to God and repent of the way I had seen myself. I could feel his pain as he looked over me with such love and pride, just as a loving father is of his children. He saw so much more in me than I ever could.

I had never seen myself belonging to anybody, but at that moment, I had a revelation that everything that I was had been thought of, planned, and created by the God of the universe. Regardless of how I felt about myself, I was no accident. I wanted to stay in that moment forever. What I had experienced was both indescribable and undeniable. It was like nothing else I had felt before. For the first time, I experienced a sense of hope. Hope that there was someone much greater than me and my efforts.

As I reflect on that evening, it is clear to me that God knew that if I were to travel the recovery journey, I would need a solid foundation. Before any of the broken pieces could be put back together, I needed to know that God had made me, and most of all, HE LOVED ME.

I woke with a new excitement stirring in my heart. I knew I had a long journey ahead of me, but I now knew I was no mistake, and God loved what he had made. I started to think that maybe God had made me with a purpose in mind.

As I opened my bible to read before the first of the volunteers arrived for breakfast, the words on the page leapt out; *"I am fearfully and wonderfully made."**

Tears fell onto my bible as I read God's word being spoken over me again. His word backed all that I felt the night before.

How amazing that he knew that those three words He spoke would anchor the battle that lay ahead for me in all my chaos? *Jesus loved me.*

I was keen for the volunteers to arrive that morning. I wanted to share with them the word I had received from God. However, I didn't want to say too much, as I was scared they would think I was now okay and leave me to battle alone. I knew I needed their support more than ever. But, on the other hand, I still wasn't ready to let go of the control.

I had decided I would gain another kilo, but this was all I was willing to allow. Of course, Sandra and Sascha had other plans, but I wasn't prepared to tell them that I wouldn't go beyond what I had settled in my mind.

I continued through my days the best I could. I continued to swap food and cheat where I could, but it seemed harder than before.

Cheating and lying seemed to conflict with the experience I'd had with God. Everything I felt with Him was safe and full of hope, but doing the wrong thing left me feeling convicted. I would justify my actions by telling myself it was to protect me. I couldn't lose control; I couldn't go back to the person I was. I didn't like who I once was. I didn't want to be that people pleaser.

> *DIARY ENTRY*
> *God, I don't want to be without the anorexia and then risk being labeled something else. At least with the anorexia, I can control how I see myself and what I think others see. If I feel threatened that I'm being labeled as something else (bossy, boring, know-all, one-eyed), I can easily control my eating and just remain the "anorexic." So, if I'm not "being" anorexic, then I feel I need to be something else, and, in my mind, it has to be something good. Therefore I just people-please. It's one or the other, and if I'm not doing the anorexic thing with my food, then I can't claim to be the anorexic- so who am I?)*

All I had to hang on to was the word I got from God. Hearing His voice now confirmed that He wasn't just a song on a Sunday, but I just wasn't sure where to put Him.

One evening after I had eaten my evening meal with the volunteer, we sat down to chat together. Cathy was a friend I had gone through school with. One of the rules for volunteering for the program was that they were not close friends or family. Although Cathy and I had been close, we had slowly lost touch as I slowly spiralled into the grips of anorexia and became isolated and withdrawn. It had been decided that she could be part of the support team.

I always knew Cathy went to church, even when we were in school, so I felt comfortable talking to her about God and was keen to share what I'd heard God say to me. After telling her what had happened that night in my room, I said, 'I know Jesus has the answer for me.'

She replied, 'Jesus doesn't just have the answer. Jesus IS your answer.'

From Sandra: *During the program, Lesley would often feel distressed that she was losing control of things. This frightened her. However, surely to have control is to have a choice. While under the grip of anorexia, she might feel like she has control, but in reality, Lesley didn't feel free just to eat if she wanted to. Anorexia was controlling her. To give it up, was to create a choice for herself and gain true control. As such, I would often reassure Lesley with the following statement:*

"As you feel you are losing control, you're actually in truth, gaining it."

Another area of struggle was the influence of woman's magazines and the photos of models in these. Lesley would compare herself to these 'air-brushed' photos and feel the need to be slimmer. The distortion of her self-image was so strong that she would feel bigger than these models when, in fact, most of them would weigh at least 20kg more than her. I advised her not to buy magazines for a while, and this seemed to help reduce her anxiety.

You are Lesley

Most people in my life believed I was too fragile to upset, confront, or challenge. I had remained in what I thought to be my safe cocoon for ten years, and the only way I knew to have any boundaries was to continue as the sick anorexic girl.

To anyone else looking in, they would see anorexia as a horrible noose around my neck, but I believed that it was the only way I could avoid confronting issues in life.

I had become complacent with being anorexic. Anorexia had become my identity. The person I once was and terrified about becoming again had long gone and left me feeling like I would never be anything more than an anorexic. The term, 'once an anorexic, always an anorexic' had even been spoken over me many times.

What hope did I have? I now knew God loved me, but I wasn't even sure who I was.

My life had just become an existence.

I was still working, and the volunteers continued to sit with me and encourage me. The words God had spoken to me were well and truly embedded in my heart, and I couldn't stop thinking about them. Over and over, they resonated within me, 'Jesus loves ME.'

After this revelation, I found my thoughts contemplating ideas and dreams I hadn't thought of for many years. Did God have a plan and a purpose for me?

Again, hope filled my heart, and for a moment, I held a glimmer of hope. I saw myself happy and whole—a life with friendships and socialising. Would I marry one day and possibly have children of my own?

Before I could dream any further, my heart felt heavy and burdened.

I could hear nothing but That tormenting voice in my head.

"You will be lost without Anorexia."

"You will have no identity."

My hope turned to hopelessness. I went from dreaming of a future and a purpose to carrying the world on my shoulder. Without the Anorexia, I would be throwing 10years away-years of striving to achieve a level of control and perfection, being sheltered from a world that just seemed incredibly scary and unsafe. This idea terrified me and left me feeling vulnerable.

Just as I was about to burst into tears, I heard that gentle voice again. 'You are Lesley.'

As I heard those words spoken, I felt the warmth and safety I felt the night in my room. A sense of peace poured over me, and every battling thought seemed to vanish.

Yes, it was my name, the name I'd been given since birth, but this was different. This was the creator of His work, declaring his ownership of his masterpiece.

I was no accident. He had created me with a unique personality. He knew what He was doing when He placed inside me the likes and dislikes, the gifts, talents, and even desires that I have. I had bottled her up for so many years and had despised so many aspects of who Lesley was.

My fear had always been either going back to the old Lesley or the anorexic Lesley, but I sensed God had something new.

This 'Lesley' he spoke of was who God had, 'fearfully and wonderfully made.' * Maybe I could get to like her? Surely it would be easier just to be who God made me to be, rather than trying to be something I wasn't? I suddenly found myself wanting to know who this Lesley was.

As I picked up my bible to read, words that I had read many times before spoke deeper into my heart. God telling me that "He knew me before I was born."*

Who is Lesley?

Something had changed. I wasn't sure what it was, but I knew for certain that I had encountered God. He was no longer just for Sundays.

He had spoken to me and had laid a firm foundation. I felt safe, and I had a desire to want to know Him more. Each time He spoke to me, I felt a peace that I'd never felt before.

Anorexia still consumed me, but I was torn between what I had experienced with God and then pleasing anorexia's voice.

One morning, as I sat with the volunteers eating breakfast, I struggled to make sense of my head's battle. The people that sat in front of me were good, honest, and caring. They had been kind to me from the beginning and continued to come and sit with me day after day.

I had always seen them as the enemy, forcing their way into my life to take something good away from me. Something I had worked so hard to gain. I thought for a moment about the previous ten years that had passed. My life was nothing more than an existence. I was terrified of losing control, but I held this new hope that maybe life could be better. I started to think that maybe what the volunteers were trying to take away from me was terrible, and they were trying to give me something better?

I tried to shake off that thought as it only represented me giving in and letting the anorexia down, but I was tired. I was tired of remaining the anorexic, and God had called me by name. I wanted to know who this Lesley was.

I began to wonder—what if I were to work with the volunteers, rather than against them? I knew there and then that it wasn't going to be easy. I knew I would be going against everything that anorexia was. But, I felt ready to take the risk. Maybe if I just took one step at a time and did not think too far ahead, I could run back if it got too hard?

Sascha, Sandra, and Bruce had set a new weight for me to reach. It was more than I had initially agreed on, but I had decided that maybe I would give it a go while working with the volunteers.

The revelation that God had made me and He loved Lesley made me keen to find out who this Lesley was?

As I would listen to conversations, I began to role play in my mind and imagined what Lesley would say if she were true to herself. The more I did this, the more I gained confidence in who I was and what I believed. As I began to understand more about myself, I began to feel more confident to speak out what I felt and thought. I didn't question whether it was right or wrong; it was me. It was who God had made; how could it be wrong?

I was usually the one to agree with everyone, too afraid to have my own opinion. I was addicted to people-pleasing and always trying so hard to say the right thing. I now felt like I had a new voice and my own opinion. I was beginning to listen to what the heart of me truly was. The more I did this, the more I trusted this Lesley that God had created and loved. I wasn't laughed at or rejected for what I had to say to my great surprise.

I remember having a conversation with one of my work colleagues and not agreeing with a topic discussed. Usually, I would have just agreed with her as I would never want to upset or hurt anyone's feelings. I would only feel safe to say what I thought they wanted to hear. I would bottle up all my feelings and beliefs, too afraid of being rejected for having a different opinion. But, I felt different this time. If God loved Lesley, I also needed to like her.

Before I could think about it anymore, from my mouth came, 'I don't agree!'

I was shocked that those words had come out of my mouth, and I could see, she was also a little surprised.

By the time I got home, I was convinced that I had utterly offended her, and my mind raced with thoughts of rejection and disapproval from her. I had concluded in my mind that she would probably never want to speak to me again. I was not looking forward to working the next day as I had anticipated an icy reception. I had already decided that I would cut back on some food today. I believed I would be safer as an anorexic rather than being labelled bossy and opinionated.

I couldn't stand that thought, and my mind battled as I considered the program and the volunteers, but I just couldn't deal with people not approving of me.

When I eventually got to work, I was greeted the same as every other morning. But, to my surprise and relief, nothing had changed between us. On the contrary, I felt something had changed for the better between us.

I believed I would be rejected if I spoke from my heart, and no one would be my friend. Remaining in a people-pleasing mindset had driven me to a place of isolation, as I believed it was the only way I could be safe.

I had to ask myself if I could be true to myself and in relationships, did that mean it was one less reason I needed the Anorexia? I knew that there could be times when I could say something that could offend someone, but I was sort of okay with that for the first time in my life. Not in an arrogant way, but because I now knew that God had made me, and He loved me.

I would speak to Sandra on most days. She would encourage me when I was down, and she celebrated my progress. I was keen to share with her what I had come to understand this day. She then asked me a question that challenged me. She wondered why I always referred to the old Lesley as a people pleaser. She asked me why I had never thought of myself as having a gift of mercy. Whenever I thought back to the old Lesley, those mocking voices would tell me everything I was, had been a negative thing. I had never thought about them being positive—a gift from God.

What else had I listened to? What else had God given to me, and I had allowed it to become something I had despised?

> **From Sandra** *One of the challenges was talking to Lesley about her lies, yet they gripped her soul. She would believe that if she ate just a little bit extra than usual, her weight would balloon, and she'd have no control of her eating at all. As in, swing from one way of eating right to the other end of the scale. I would reassure her that this wouldn't happen, but I would also say that she would never be fully convinced until she stepped out and did eat more and see. She needed to prove it for herself. Lesley would predict that she would feel awful about eating more or gaining weight but was always pleasantly surprised that when she did take the step and see, that it was nothing like she had imagined.*

ANOREXIA EXPOSED

With my 6 sisters (L-R: Sue, Lynn, Fiona, Robyn, Barbara, Lesley and Vicky)

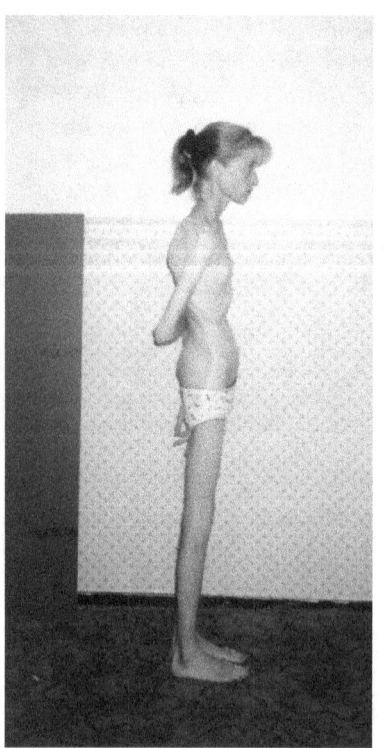

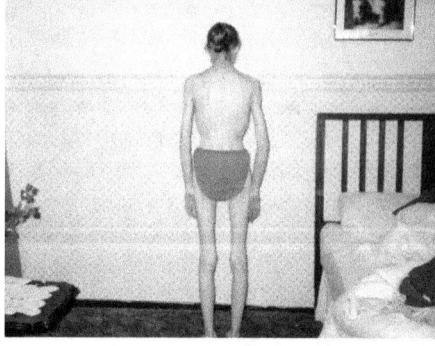

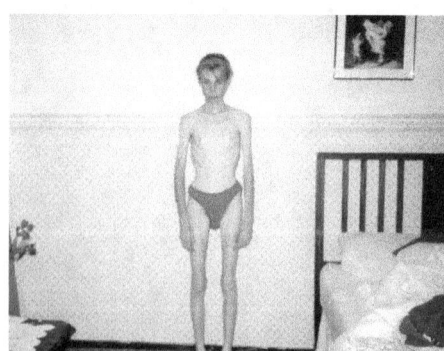

Above & Right: Me, 23 years old just prior to recovery intervention.

PHOTOS

On my wedding day with Mum and Dad.

John & I on our wedding day.

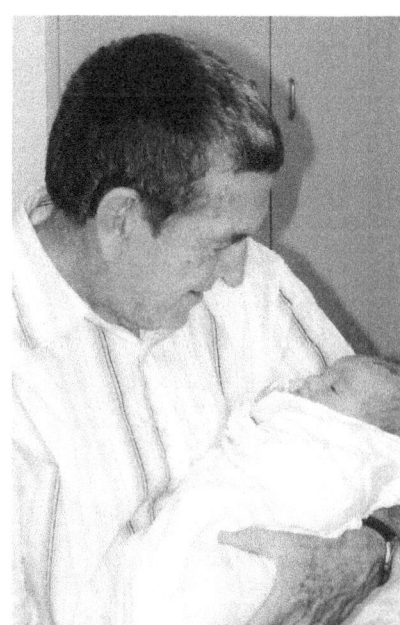
Dad (Ted) proudly holding my son Riley

ANOREXIA EXPOSED

Happy and pregnant with my daughter Ella.

My Mum (Sheila) with Ella.

With my daughter Ella.

PHOTOS

Road to Recovery

This is an agreement between Lesley Sharon Morris and her assistants in her Road to Recover from her Anorexia.

The three primary assistants are
Sascha ▓▓▓▓▓▓▓▓
Sandra ▓▓▓▓▓
Bruce ▓▓▓▓▓▓

Other assistants will be recruited and named on the attached schedule of volunteers.

The primary goal of this program is that Lesley achieves an initial goal weight of 35kg. This goal weight may be revised form time to time by the Core Carers group.

The Core Carers group presently comprises Lesley, Sascha, Sandra and Bruce.

Lesley agrees to
    In general, comply with the decisions of the Core Carers group
    Specifically
        to relinquish control over decisions as to her food intake
        To allow Volunteer Carers to be in her presence at times decided by the Core Carers group
        Comply with Core Carers group decisions as to work and exercise and other aspects of her lifestyle as appropriate.

Sandra's responsibilities comprise in general, Dietetics
    Specifically
        Dietary planning
        Reviews of diet including increments
        Reviewing weight and biochemical results from time to time
        Coordinating dietary matters with Lesley and Volunteer Carers

Sascha's responsibilities comprise
        Recruiting and coordinating Volunteer Carers
        Time tabling Volunteers
        Mediating problems from Volunteers and routing these to Sandra &/or Bruce

Bruce's responsibilities comprise
        Overall monitoring and good management of the program
        Consulting as appropriate with outside professionals including Lesley's GP
        Coordinating with outside groups including work group and family group
        Responsible to see that problems with volunteers are solved in consultation with Core Carers

Volunteer Carers responsibilities comprise
        Work with Lesley according to roster

        Commit to attend with Lesley at designated times
        Work only within the therapy guidelines as prescribed in the Recovery Program
        Initiate no spontaneous therapy ideas other than those in the Program
        Refer all problems to Volunteer Coordinator for solution and reporting
        Read and adhere to written Volunteer Procedures

The contract between myself, Sascha, Sandra and Bruce for the recovery program.

Forgiving my Way to Freedom

I could not believe that six months along with the recovery program's commencement, both myself and the volunteers remained.

However, two compelling, life-changing revelations had kept me from giving up: First, Jesus loved me, and secondly, He called me by name, Lesley.

Sandra would continue to encourage and speak into my life. As my journey evolved, she would continuously guide me with words of wisdom and grace. She was only ever a phone call away, and I never felt that there was ever any judgment.

One day she phoned me and began to share what she believed to be a vital part of my continuing journey toward recovery.

She continued to explain the power of forgiveness and challenged me with any unforgiveness I may have in my heart. She proceeded to tell me that forgiveness was not only about forgiving those that you feel may have hurt you but also those that I may have hurt. She suggested that I make a list with everyone's name on it that I needed to forgive and those I required forgiveness.

Anorexia is a destructive battle for the sufferer and those close to them. My family had endured years of helplessly watching someone they loved and, once enjoyed, slowly self-destruct.

I justified my actions, decisions, and behaviours with blame.

I didn't wholly understand why Sandra would have me do what she was asking, but I trusted her and was desperate to do what I could if it meant any recovery chance.

It wasn't an easy task. I sat down, listed names on paper, and set about what I needed to do. I had remembered back to a sermon I had heard at church. Explaining that forgiveness wasn't based on how you felt; instead, it was based on a choice to obey God, and forgiveness is what God asks of us.*

If I had based forgiveness on how I felt, I would not have done anything. My feelings were bogged in past hurts, blame, and self- pity. I believed that recovery was only possible if everyone else changed.

I knew that I had to trust what God's word said.

I arranged to catch up with several people I knew I needed to forgive and seek forgiveness. I didn't experience any life-changing moments, but as the days passed, I began to feel like something had shifted and changed. I couldn't put my finger on it, but I held more hope for moving forward. The condemning voice of anorexia seemed quieter?

It had been so emotionally tiring to carry around my hurts and believe my only hope for recovery was everyone else changing. I knew that as I chose to forgive them and for them to forgive me, I had set them free, but I had unblocked a road, and I was now free to travel it.

The deep, toxic root of anorexia was slowly being exposed and removed.

Spirit and Flesh

It had been close to nine months into the recovery program, and I found myself in a place I had never anticipated, nor a place I could ever have dreamed. I had this hope that I had never experienced, and I was beginning to believe that maybe I could live a life free of anorexia for the first time in many years.

I still had many pieces missing from the puzzle and wasn't yet convinced that I was safe without anorexia.

I remembered back to Bruce's initial comment, describing anorexia as an "addiction." He was right. I was addicted to this cycle of fear and starvation.

Every day brought a whole new set of challenges with it, whether physical, emotional, or psychological. I battled daily, but the volunteers continued to arrive every day, speaking words of life and hope. They would avoid speaking about anorexia. Instead, talk about what life could look like, painting a picture of a world outside of anorexia.

With their unconditional love and support, it seemed only fair that I make as much of an effort as I possibly could. My weight had already passed the initial weight goal, and even though I was terrified of gaining too much, I tried to take one day at a time.

Having had God's word spoken to me directly, I felt this unexplained peace and trust that I'd never before experienced.*

When I could get away with cheating, I would still take advantage of the situation. I really couldn't make sense of why I did what I did.

Why was it so tough to do the right thing?

I was addicted to worry. I would wake each morning, asking myself,

'What do I need to be worrying about today?'

If nothing came straight to mind, I would look for something.

Surely, there must be something for me to worry about?

Everything I tried to make positive, the anorexia would convince me otherwise. Surely, if I ate any food that was outside my safe list, I would lose complete control? Surely, if I didn't stay in complete control, my weight would soar?
Surely, if I got too close to people, they would find out what I was really like and not want to be my friend?
It was all lies, but I was like a puppet on a string.
One evening, as I buried my head in my bible, I was drawn to read through the scriptures. The words began to speak to my heart:
I do not understand what I do. For what I want to do,
I do not do, but what I hate I do.
For I have the desire to do what is good, but I cannot carry it out.*
As I finished reading the scripture, I knew that God had led me to answer the question I'd been struggling with, 'Why do I do what I do?'
I had asked that question so many times over the last ten years. I was always trying to figure out the answer. Why? Why did I continue to do what I did when I knew it wasn't good? Although I loved my family, Why did I continue to punish them through my choices to self-destruct?
So much of what I did, didn't make sense, but no matter how I thought about it, no matter how hard I tried, no matter how many times I'd been told, it didn't change anything. I was still left with the same questions, 'Why do I do what I do?' 'Why is it a battle?'
I had read this scripture in the Bible so many times, but I could never make sense of all the do's!
This time it was different. It was as though the scripture jumped out of the pages. I began to read how God had made us both *flesh and spirit*.
The flesh side of us was all about ourselves. Everything the flesh desires is to please only its-self. The spirit in us is God in us, and the spirit wants to please God.
I could now see that I had a battle on my hands. It was natural for the flesh to rebel against what the spirit wanted. Finally, it was starting to make sense. Now I understood why it seemed such a battle to do what was right. God designed us to serve and please him, but we are made up of a body(Flesh) that only wants to do what we want to do and to satisfy our selfish desires. I realised it was natural to struggle to do the right thing to not rely on feelings.
This was not news to God. He was completely aware of this daily battle we have, but I knew He wanted me to see that He was always there to help me decide and make the right decision. I had battled for so many years, being dictated to by what I was feeling at any given moment. This night, I realised another way, but not necessarily a natural way. There wasn't anything wrong with me. I wasn't a bad person. However, I was allowing myself to be dictated by my flesh/self's desires,

which I now understood, would lead only to death. I now had an alternative: listening to what God(spirit) was saying, which would lead to life.

This wasn't about how good I was or about my willpower, nor was it about how I was feeling at the time. *

I had often heard it preached at church about the 'enemy,' 'Satan,' or 'the devil.' But was he a real force? Was the "voices of anorexia" his voice?

Surely, I was smart enough not to follow Satan and see his evil?

I remembered a phone call from Sandra a few weeks earlier. She had called me and asked me if I had ever questioned those voices and thoughts in my head? She had said that sometimes what we think to be our thoughts can be lies whispered to us from the enemy?

It now was making more sense.

If God had made me, liked what He made, and called me by name, I could trust the spirit inside me. I could see now that there would always be the flesh in me that is all about self, but I didn't have to feel and act on it.

Before developing anorexia, I had this unrealistic desire to be perfect. I couldn't cope with the thought of not getting life right. I was afraid of upsetting people, saying the wrong thing, or exposing any flaws. Eventually, this expectation was too much for me. Anorexia had offered me a way out. It was my way of saying, 'I'm not perfect.' It made me believe that I had a free pass to have all expectations removed the skinnier or more unwell I became.

To now read that God is aware that we are not perfect and won't ever be, as we are both spirit (complete) and flesh (imperfect, unspiritual) was so refreshing to know.

The enemy had screamed this expectation to be perfect at me, knowing too well that it was impossible and would lead me to self-destruct.

As the program continued, I was more than aware that my recovery chances were only possible if I continued to get closer to God and what His word (Bible) had to say.

Although anxious about what lay ahead, I found myself with a new focus. Every spare moment I had, I would ponder on all that God had spoken to me.

I continued flicking through my Bible with excitement. I wanted to absorb more and more of what God had to say. My eyes then caught these words, *"Noone can serve two masters"* *

I knew that God was referring to Himself and Anorexia.

It was as though a light shone on that passage, and I knew I couldn't read on any further. It was another moment of God revealing Himself and His truth to me. Everything God had shown me was safe, comforting, and lovely to hear until this point. He had shown me His love, had spoken my name. He had revealed the battle I had was real, but now He was exposing a hard truth. I knew he was presenting a reality that was hard to hear and act on.

There was no denying what God had spoken to me up to now. Every word and revelation bought so much comfort and reassurance, but I had continued to serve the anorexia first and foremost. God had remained in second place. Anorexia had absorbed every area of my life, and I had become a slave to it. I would bow down to its every request. Anorexia was my master. How could I completely obey and serve God when my body and mind were still a slave to anorexia?

I loved God. Every encounter revealed a God full of love, kindness, patience, and grace. I wanted to serve Him, but I was now aware that I would have to lay anorexia down to give God first place.

I could feel God's heart, just like the evening I first heard him tell me He loved me. He had already shown me his intentions for my life. He loved me, and His heart was for me to be free, to be the Lesley He had created. I could feel the ache in His heart, yet he was so gracious and patient with my readiness. I continued reading, His word confirming all that I felt. *

I then came to five words that jumped out at me,

'*I am a jealous God.*' I knew what God was asking. I was terrified, but I had to trust this God that had gently and ever so graciously got me to this point.

My battle with anorexia had created an all-or-nothing mentality. Daily rituals and habits drove me. It not only gave me a sense of control, but it pleased the anorexia. It would prove that I was its greatest follower and the obsessive nature of anorexia. I would have to eat from the same cup, use the same bowl every morning for breakfast, and smell everything a certain amount of times before eating it to savor the limited eating experience. I was obsessed with the levels I would pour into a cup or using the same spoon to measure quantities. I would purchase the same food brands and never consider an alternative. I resented eating out socially, as I did not want to detour from my set daily food intake.

I now knew that this was all part of me "serving" the anorexia master, and God was now asking me to serve Him. I was scared, but I had no doubt what God was asking of me.

I was anxious about losing control, but I was beginning to ask myself whether the anorexia controlled me?

Addicted to Control

The program had been running for around one year, and still, the volunteers continued to come and support me. I appreciated them more than ever, as I knew their support and accountability were essential for moving forward.

Everyone involved was happy with the progress so far, although I still had a way to go. I could not deny the hand God had on my life and the work He was doing. As God continued to speak revelation and truth into my life, the temptation and desire to turn back to anorexia began to look less appealing. Although I was now aware of God's desire for me to lay down the anorexia and serve Him, He knew exactly when and what to speak and when to show me. He knew there were so many facets and layers of anorexia and what kept me hanging on to it, so I was so grateful that I was learning to serve a God who was not impatient or pushy.

As I tried to think more about what God had spoken to me, rather than listen to the anorexia, I could continue to push through my fears. I became more honest with all involved in my recovery, as I knew I needed to expose the lies and have them support what I found so hard to do and overcome.

Sandra encouraged me to imagine and picture myself doing certain things that I had been too afraid to do. She said that she understood I might not be quite ready to do it, but visualizing myself doing these things would help me become familiar with them and turn them into possible rather than impossible. God knew how hard every little step was for me, but as I trusted and served Him, He would replace it with so much more. He never made me give anything up and leave me with a void but would exchange it with something so much better: truth and freedom.

One Sunday at church, I was invited to a birthday party. Ten years of anorexia were ten years of isolation and loneliness. I had become so detached from normal, and even if someone attempted to include me, I would only decline. I would see it as a possibility to lose control. I had been a slave to this lie and had allowed so much to be robbed from me.

I knew God would want me to say yes, so I decided to face my fears and accept the invitation.

I drove to the party with both nerves and anticipation. It had been a long time since I had been in a social setting and had no idea what to expect. Sandra had suggested that I eat my planned dinner before I leave, then I need not worry about what to eat while out and possibly be tempted to eat nothing.

When I arrived, I could see some familiar faces from church, but most of them were only that, as I had never really made an effort to get to know anyone. However, it wasn't long before someone came up to me, and we started a conversation. The night went by quickly, and I was pleased I had made an effort to meet some new people. As I left the party, one of the guys said that he was not familiar with the area and could follow me to the main road.

We headed down the hill, and he followed behind. When we had reached the main road, he accelerated alongside my car and signalled for me to pull over. He rolled his window down and asked if I would be keen to join him for a late-night hot chocolate at the nearest café. It was getting late, and I was a little dumbfounded by his request. It had been a considerably long time since I had been asked to join someone for a catch-up, more so by a male! Nevertheless, I decided to say yes, so I followed him to the nearest coffee shop.

I wasn't sure what to think as I drove along behind him. My perception of who I was had been tipped upside down and shaken. On the other hand, I was encouraged that what God had been speaking to me about was being reinforced. We pulled into the cafe, and I quickly searched the glove box. I found an old battered lipstick, so I decided to apply some to my lips.

We sat and talked for a couple of hours, trying to appear normal and comfortable in this very uncomfortable position I'd found myself in. I didn't even know what to order but figured it was easiest to order whatever he ordered. I later drove home in disbelief. Yet, I could sense God with me, and I knew He wanted to show me the road of life and not death.

Maybe life wasn't so scary after all?

God was opening the doors of life as I chose to close the doors of anorexia.

When I arrived home, I was eager to journal. There was so much going around in my head, and I needed to put pen to paper. There was an excitement I hadn't experienced in a long time. I suddenly found myself wanting to embrace life.

I looked into the mirror and found myself wanting to look better. My clothes were still a little baggy, and my face a little gaunt. Anorexia never held back, reminding me of all my flaws and how worthless I was. Anorexia had praised me the more I deprived and punished myself physically and emotionally. I now had my creator telling me I was loved, planned, and I needed to now choose either God (life) or anorexia (death), but I couldn't have both.

I wanted to serve God, and I knew God was asking me to lay some things down that only represented me being a slave to anorexia, and I now needed to choose God. For the first time, I dared to dream about looking after my appearance and taking care of my body. I could barely contain my excitement as I contemplated all the beautiful things I hadn't done for such a long time. Having my hair styled, shopping for new clothes, applying makeup, and enjoying all those things that women should experience.

Then without warning, heaviness and fear consumed me. My excitement and dreams for the future dissolved.

All I could hear in my head was, 'You can't look better. If you look better, everyone will think you are well, and they will dump all their problems on you again. You will be vulnerable."

At this point, I was a slave again to anorexia, and my hope had disappeared. There was a battle going on in my head. God said, 'You can,' and the anorexia was shouting, 'You can't.'

I felt defeated, but I had this greater sense that God was waiting for something. Just as I was about to throw in the towel and give in to the anorexia, I felt God ask me, 'Why do you want to look so unwell and sick?'

It was as though someone had just pulled back some heavy block out curtains in a pitch-black room. I could see it as clear as if God was standing before me speaking it to me. The truth was: I didn't want to look better because I didn't want to lose control.

This was not about anyone ELSE; this was about ME. I had mastered this control over everyone else. While I remained looking so sick and unwell, I believed I could control all of those around me. If anything was said to upset me, I could lose more weight, which would be my way of punishing them, and in turn, I would feel I could control their reactions and responses to me.

Anorexia kept me sitting in the driver's seat of control and manipulation. I had come to believe this was the only way to keep myself from offenses, hurt, rejection, and people's responses. As long as I listened to the anorexia, it was an excuse for me to live with self-pity and blame.

I could not deny what God was asking of me that evening. He was resetting me on the inside, and it was time to start showing this on the outside.

He did not want me to use anything or anyone to cope with living my life. Instead, he wanted me to trust Him with the person He had made—Lesley.

A moment of truth and revelation hit me like a wave. I dropped to my knees amongst the pile of clothes I had been trying on and sobbed. I knew that this would mean having to hand the control over to God and allow people to choose to like me or not? Usually, this would have terrified me and would be an unbearable thought to contemplate, but I sensed God telling me, 'Set them free and be free".

Although I had come to know and love God more, this was a huge step and risk. For years, the anorexia had convinced me that the only way to remain safe was to listen to its every instruction, but I now had to face what God had exposed and face the truth behind my motivations.

I had to listen now, obey, and trust God with another layer of anorexia He was peeling away.

I loved that God was interested in restoring all parts of me to bring about wholeness, spiritually, emotionally, and physically.

Although my appearance would typically only represent a physical change, God knew it would also be an opportunity to expose an emotional and spiritual discovery. It exposed another lie that anorexia told me for all these years. I had no choice but to see it for what it had become to me and what God could see. He wanted better for me; he wanted me free.

I took the physical change and weight gain day by day. I tried not to think too far ahead and focus on Sandra's small weight gain goals before me. I realised once again how vital the support of every volunteer around me was as they encouraged and prayed for me as I took each step forward. One of the volunteers took me shopping to buy myself some new clothes and allowed me to feel what it was like to be kind to myself and be okay with that.

It wasn't long before the physical evidence of my journey to recovery was getting noticed. I was entirely out of my comfort zone, but I was beginning to understand that I was allowing God to be in control whenever I felt out of control. I began to crave being out of control, as I knew that God would always meet me. *

One day at work, a patient arrived that I hadn't seen since her last visit to us six months earlier. I bought her into the clinic and sat her down, sitting opposite her. As I began to talk with her as I usually would, I noticed her looking at me with a curious look. She paused for a moment and then asked me, 'Are you related to Lesley?' I was a little confused with why she would ask me that, so I responded with, 'I am Lesley.'

God was changing me from the inside out. He had assured me that He had made me. I wasn't the anorexic nor the broken Lesley I viewed myself to be. He was only asking me to be Lesley He had made, and I was learning to be okay with that.

DIARY ENTRY
Well, I'm off to a social night to try my "first" real pizza. Sandra and I have talked about it, and I feel it's the right thing to do. Even though it would be easier and safer to eat my own food before I go, and I could just say that id already eaten, but there is a part of me that wants to join in and be a part. God, please help me. I do expect to feel uncomfortable, but as long as I know it's all for good and I will be okay and I will even come out the better

for it. There is something frustrating about just being safe and doing the same thing! I know this will result in many different benefits that I just can't see yet? There is something good about doing what "I" want to do instead of doing what my mind (anorexia) tries to tell me to do.

Mind your Own Business

My Saturday mornings were like every other day, with one of the volunteers coming to sit with me for breakfast. In addition, Helen would often bring study material from her mid-week Bible study to share with me. I became desperate to learn more of God's word and learn more about him, so I looked forward to our Saturday morning catch-ups.

One morning, she shared a scripture passage discussed earlier in her week with me. She began reading from the book of John in the Bible.*

After reading, Helen explained the passage and gave me a picture of the scenario between Jesus and Simon Peter. She spoke about how Jesus seemed to keep persisting with asking him if Simon Peter loved Him and, in the end, Simon Peter points at the disciple and tries to deflect the attention and says, 'What about him?

I enjoyed sharing God's word with Helen, and from the passage, I could relate to God, asking me to lay down the anorexia and follow Him. I now knew I could say, "Yes, I love you, Lord," and was now conscious of serving Him and not the anorexia.

I continued without much further thought about what we had read together in the morning throughout my day.

Later that afternoon, I decided to go over to my parent's home and spend some time with them. Between working and my commitment to the program, I hadn't spent as much time over at their home. My time with them certainly wasn't as strained now, but I was still learning to establish myself as Lesley and not the anorexic.

We headed out for an afternoon drive together. From the time we had left the house, I felt unsettled but could not put my finger on what was wrong.

Typically, when I was with my family, I saw myself as the victim. I would drag myself around in a cocoon of self-pity and look to them to fix my horrible predicament. I had learned to shut myself off from the world around me and indeed to anyone else's needs or feelings, and I believed I had every excuse. If I didn't feel in control, I had become an expert at using anorexia to control the situation by playing the victim.

This behaviour would only ever result in the other person feeling guilty, and I would get my way, and in turn, feel in control. It was a horrible cycle of manipulation, guilt, and fear, but one I had become completely addicted to.

This day was different. I was now so acutely aware of God exposing my motives and now being unable to hide behind the anorexia. I felt exposed and vulnerable. No longer could I manipulate and control what people thought of me. I had to allow them the freedom to choose. I knew this meant I had to let go and trust God, but I didn't like how I felt.

I was now feeling vulnerable. I had spent years controlling relationships with anorexia, but I now had to trust God and step back.

I felt physically sick. It was as though a spotlight shone on me, and I had nowhere to run. Mum and dad continued to talk to me, but I couldn't hear anything they were saying. All I could hear were words of disapproval from the anorexia,

'You are weak.'

'Your parents won't love you as much if you're not so sick.'

'You have no control.'

It went on and on in my head until I couldn't take it anymore. I knew what God had said and asked of me, but it all seemed too hard.

I told Mum and Dad I wanted to go home and held back tears. Of course, they had no idea what was going on, but my irrational outbursts were not uncommon to them that they asked no questions, and we headed back to their home.

I got straight back into my car and drove home. It felt like walls were coming in on me, and I was suffocating.

I began to cry out to God and question what was going on. Why would he bring me this far and then leave me feeling so exposed and vulnerable?

I felt as if everyone else had got their way, and I was the one feeling left with this person 'Lesley', who I still don't even know that well.

Why would God do that?

Before I could feel any sorrier for myself, I heard these words inside my heart:

'Mind your own business.'

I sat back in the car seat and wiped the tears from my eyes. I heard, clearly and firmly, but spoken with love and grace, God's voice, and felt that overwhelming sense of peace once again.

I felt no sense of guilt or shame; I saw truth through God's eyes.

I felt convicted, but at the same time, God's love and grace were so overwhelming. So I didn't say anything to God but drove quietly as I soaked up the reality of His truth and discipline. He had set me free from this burden of carrying everyone else's troubles but had exposed my pride at thinking it was my job.

Truth and freedom were held in those four simple words. "Mind your own business."

God had never asked me to focus on everyone else around me. How much easier would it be if I just took care of MY own business? I could see it was another level of my control. I had wanted to mind everyone else's business, as I believed it gave me a sense of power, but again this was only for my benefit. God was now disciplining me to lay it down and focus on what He was only asking of me.

I finally reached home and was more desperate than ever to write in my journal and open my Bible. Again, His word confirmed all that I had heard and felt. *

The enemy had known that if he could get me believing it was my job to fix everything and everyone, it would eventually lead me to become resentful, bitter, and ultimately self-destruct.

But God had never asked this of me.

No person could have said those words to me and had the impact and revelation it had in my life but God. *

I began to understand that my recovery journey would not be just about all the gentle, kind, and encouragement from God. But, still, I needed to accept His discipline also.

He loved me too much to leave any room for the enemy to come back in. So I could see why He spoke His love to me right at the beginning. He knew that I needed to know He was a loving father that I could trust.

He is in Control

By this stage of the program, I had come to a place of complete reliance on God. I knew only by His grace could I overcome anorexia completely. I refused to believe that once an anorexic, always an anorexic. God loved me and had called me by name, "Lesley." His plan for me was wholeness, freedom, and joy.

I was desperate to hear as much of God's word as I could get. I wanted to hear and learn as much as possible, as I knew this was my hope for freedom. My rituals and obsession with food were becoming less important. I would eat my last meal for the day with a volunteer in the evening, and as soon as they would leave, I would read my Bible or watch Christian teaching videos.

As it had now been around fifteen months since the recovery program had commenced, it was only natural that the intensity of the support had tapered down, but a core group remained. I did all that was within my power to ensure the volunteers continued, as I was aware of their support more than ever. I would now often take my meals to their home to eat with them and, in turn, was welcomed into many families.

On one of my weekly counselling sessions with Bruce, he had asked if my immediate family could join me. During this session, Bruce was keen to fill the family in on my progress. After answering the family's questions, he then turned to me. He requested I position each family member in a physical line to represent the order I would like us to now function as a family? First, who would lead, and then those that would follow? I wasn't entirely sure what Bruce was expecting to achieve out of this activity, but I trusted Bruce and was willing to do what he was asking?

As I began to physically position each family member in the order of my preference, I realised how emotionally difficult this would be. I placed Mum and Dad together at the top of the room. I began to experience feelings that I hadn't anticipated as I did this. For so many years, I had taken it upon myself to be my mum's ears and eyes. I saw myself knowing best and believing that Mum needed me or she wouldn't cope. I left no room for Dad and certainly no room for God. Never had Mum asked me to take on the role, but I had convinced myself that Mum needed me.

I positioned us all in a straight line with all six sisters, side by side. Equal.

It wasn't an easy session for me. As I looked around the room and saw each of us positioned, tears streamed down my face. I had taken it upon myself to push myself to the top, but it was not the order in which God had intended and, in turn, had resulted in me self-destructing.

It was a powerful moment as I took my rightful place.

As I drove home, I thanked God for showing me the keys to unlocking the chains that held me in the cycle of anorexia. I asked Him to comfort me as I struggled with so many emotions and feelings about what I had done. What if I had said the wrong thing? What if I should have positioned everyone differently? These thoughts consumed my mind.

I continued to talk to God. I didn't hear anything back, but I sensed a calming, and I felt God closer than ever. I then got this picture in my mind. It was a picture of Jesus nailed to the cross. I wasn't just seeing my God. I was seeing Jesus. The Jesus I had got to know more and more over the last year and a half. The Jesus who personally spoke His love for me, the Jesus that made me and named me, the Jesus who showed me life when the anorexia screamed death.

My heart was breaking as I saw Jesus nailed to the cross. Why was I being shown this?

In my heart, I got these words, 'Your guilt and shame have been nailed to the cross. I did this for you.'

As I drove home that night, I began to talk to God about what had happened in Bruce's office.

The picture of Jesus on the cross then became so clear. Jesus had died, shed His blood to set me free from any guilt, shame, or whatever the enemy tried to throw at me. I got it!

This revelation had no sooner penetrated my heart when I saw a black figure dart across my car's bonnet and disappear? Before I could try and work out what it was, I remembered this scripture.

"Resist the devil, and he will flee." *

I knew that the dark figure was the enemy fleeing without any doubt.

I had received the most powerful weapon to continue fighting and overcoming this battle. Anorexia no longer stood a chance. It was as though Jesus had put a set of keys into my hand, and no one could take them off me. I had been given the keys to victory. The blood of Jesus on that cross.

Years of accusations, lies, guilt, and self-punishment. The battle had been won, and Jesus had put the keys of life into my hands. The enemy knew what I had been given that night—the revelation of the power of Jesus's blood. The power of the cross. *

The enemy was defeated, and that night he fled. The revelation I had just encountered gave the enemy less chance to torment me any further with anorexia.

Without any doubt, I knew that the dark figure I saw dart across my car was the enemy fleeing.

As I continued to drive, I laughed and cried as I soaked up what I had experienced. Then, I drove along, screaming out, 'I'm free!'

I'm sure any other drivers would have looked and thought I'd gone mad!

I felt so overwhelmed with a strength and certainty I'd never experienced before, but I felt God hadn't finished. As I drove and waited, soaking up His peace, I felt Him wanting to speak more of His word.

When I finally arrived home, I began to read from my Bible. The words I read only confirmed all that I had felt earlier.*

The enemy knew that he would now only be wasting his time with me, but where would he go? I sensed that he would soon look for other vulnerable souls to torment. Understanding the reality of how active and real this enemy was alarmed me, and I realised His ultimate plan is death.

John 10:10 The thief(devil) comes only to steal and kill and destroy, I (Jesus) have come that they may have life, and have it to the full.

For so many years, I had people consistently praying for me. Through my years of battling anorexia, my family never gave up on me. Although my situation seemed physically hopeless, they could do nothing; they were willing to pray and believe in a miracle.

Other believers knew that Jesus not only had the answer, but He was my answer. Therefore, they believed that recovery was possible if they could uphold me in prayer until I could find Jesus.

I had been lied to by the enemy for so many years.

He had led me into anorexia and continued to lie to me, keeping me a prisoner and slave to it. Anorexia was not who I was. It had come straight from the pit of hell. The devil's only intention was to steal life from me, eventually, kill me and leave a trail of destruction in its path.

I had now come to understand the power of all the prayers throughout my recovery. God was now reminding me how important and necessary prayer was in protecting others.

From Sandra: *It was so lovely to see Lesley blossom and increase in joy, confidence, and freedom. She started to take better care of herself as her self-esteem improved and depression waned.*

Her interest grew in clothes, painting her nails, and makeup. After much planning with me, she even started to venture out to social events of what she might eat there. I wanted to stretch her choices a little but not overwhelm her. She needed to eat equivalent nutrients and calories as well.

There were fears and struggles along the way of the recovery, but there were also good times. Lesley now had lots more friends and was enjoying social events. Joy and laughter were once again part of her life.

Taking Life Back

I continued receiving all the support I could get. I remembered back to the beginning of the program when Glenda told me to see this opportunity of support just as though I was receiving medical treatment on an operating table and not getting off until restoration was complete.

I was grateful to so many people who had supported me and became very close to me.

Their accountability and support were priceless, and I knew I would need it for a little longer.

Life was changing and changing for the better. I was beginning to go out more and socialise with a lot more people. I was experiencing a world I'd never seen before.

Rather than having someone meet me for breakfast in my home, we had agreed to meet once a week at a coffee shop before work, and I learned to order from a menu. I would sit amongst families and share in their meal times and conversations. One of the volunteers suggested I hold a small dinner party for her and a couple of close friends. It was quite a daunting thought, but I decided to embrace it. I had to go out and buy plates and cutlery, as I hadn't entertained before.

One of the volunteers who had many years of experience as a sports coach went out of her way to write up my exercise program. She carefully thought through a gentle start to my introduction to some daily exercise. It was so refreshing to get out each morning, smell the fresh air, and embrace a new life that I could not have ever imagined.

Bruce was happy with the results and transformation. I remember going to one weekly session, and although I was now 26 years old, he sat and listened as I excitedly told him about the past week I had enjoyed. He commented that I was currently experiencing what an eighteen-year-old should experience. The following week, I would share again what my week involved. He would then say; I was now experiencing a 21-year-olds life.

It made me think back to a time I was with one of the volunteers, and I was feeling down that ten-plus years had slipped through my fingers, and I felt I had missed out on so much because of the anorexia.

She then quoted words from the Bible about how God could restore time to us that the devil had robbed from us.

It was so very true. Although, on paper, I had lost ten years battling and suffering from anorexia, it felt as though God was now taking me through those years in a condensed space of time, and He was restoring to me those years that were a time of isolation and sadness.

I couldn't believe how different my life was. It was nothing short of a miracle. It was hard at times to think it was my life, but instead, a spectator watching somebody else. So I couldn't have been more surprised when I received a call from Bruce (psychiatrist) asking me if I would be interested in being interviewed by a television interview program. They wanted a story on eating disorders and had contacted Bruce whether he knew of anyone?

I had mixed feelings about being involved. Was I "well" enough to talk about recovery? What about all the areas that I still needed to work on? I also knew that if I made a public declaration to some "recovery," it made me accountable and would make going back even harder, and that was thought both good and scary.

At the core of my heart, I knew that I wanted to offer hope to others suffering from an eating disorder, so I decided to agree with the interview.

When the journalist came to my home to interview me, she had asked if I had any photos of myself in those dark days. I gave her what I had without thinking about going through any of them before handing them to her.

When my interview was to be aired later that week, I realised that I had given her all those sad and vulnerable photos. I knew that many people I knew, including my work colleagues, would watch the program and see those photos. The shame and embarrassment began to bombard my mind, and I wished I hadn't handed her those photos.

That evening, Glenda and Tony invited me to watch it over at their home. When the photos appeared on TV, I was surprised that I didn't feel embarrassed or ashamed. But, looking at those photos, I didn't see Lesley. For the first time, I only saw anorexia.

Although I was happy that I could finally see myself apart from the anorexia, I recall asking myself, who would ever want me? I assumed they would think I'd still be carrying so much baggage.

Caroline had been part of my recovery program and became a good friend. She invited me to one of the church Bible study groups held in someone's home once a week. Learning to socialise and mix with people was all part of my recovery journey, so I saw this as another opportunity to embrace this new path I had found myself on.

Once we arrived, I saw several familiar faces, but there was one person that I hadn't met before. John seemed friendly, but I did notice his overall knowledge of the Bible and his ability to reference Bible scriptures. I remember thinking how little of the Bible I knew and feeling a little intimidated around him.

One Sunday, after a church service, I noticed John from afar trying to get my attention. He signalled for me to come over to where he was standing. I was unsure he was referring to me, so I looked behind, but no one was behind me. Again, he signalled, so I walked over to him, although a little hesitant.

He asked me if I worked in a dental practice and whether he could get my number as he had a toothache and needed to see a dentist. As I sat down to write the number down for him, he asked me if I had any lunch plans. He caught me off guard, so I told him I had no plans and agreed to lunch with him.

He had suggested I choose where we would eat. He had no idea what a massive question this was for me. Where to eat?

Anorexia was all about isolation and deprivation. Unfortunately, I did not have a list of cafes and restaurants I had visited, but I was determined to look as normal and confident as possible.

The only problem was I didn't know what normal was or how it appeared. I was still learning to live this new life and be the Lesley God had made me. But, I knew more than ever; it was a time to trust and depend on God.

I remembered a little eatery someone from our Bible study group had mentioned. It wasn't far from the church, so I decided to choose it for us to have lunch.

After deciding what to order, we sat and waited for our lunch. When the food arrived at our table, the next difficulty was how much do I eat? All these simple, everyday activities that I had forgotten how to do.

It was easy to talk to John. We shared a lot about each of our families and the things in life that excited us. John was born in New Zealand and had moved to Australia with his family, but he had plans to travel the world.

I was intrigued with this life he shared—one of spontaneity, excitement, and freedom. But, as I sat listening, I was embarrassed with my predictable, safe, and what I believed to be a boring life. At the time, Unaware was John's thoughts of how stable and secure my life appeared, and all he was craving was his name printed in a phone book with a fixed address!

We spent the rest of the afternoon together, and the next day John called me at work to arrange another time to meet up. As John had shared so much about his future travelling plans, I believed he would not be looking for anything more than a friendship, so I felt safe to catch up with him without giving him any false messages. I certainly was not looking for any more than a friendship, and I had enjoyed John's company, so I agreed to catch up with him again.

Ironically John loved food and took much pleasure in eating a good meal any time of the day. He would often invite me over to cook for me. His meals were massive. I tried so hard to appear like I knew what I was doing, but it was all very new. We spent a lot of our time together laughing and enjoying what life had to offer. I never felt fearful, and I always had a sense of God with me. I would often debrief with Sandra the following day. I was like a baby learning to walk and eat again.

I remember one night when John had taken me to an expensive restaurant. I ordered fish from the menu. Unfortunately, it hadn't been filleted when it was delivered, so I had this whole fish sitting before me. I wanted to look confident, but I had no idea how to deal with this fish on my plate. Fortunately, John excused himself from the table to go to the men's room. At this point, I quickly asked the waitress to come over and asked her if she could brief me on how to eat this fish. By the time John returned, I was a lot more confident to eat what was before me.

It was a time of relearning, changing mindsets, and learning to trust again. Of course, I didn't always get it right, but God held my hand every step of the way.

John would later share with me that when he had watched the interview on television, he saw a woman of courage. He believed that if I could overcome anorexia, I must have a lot of strength.

I never felt different or judged by John. He didn't treat me like someone who was recovering from anorexia. On the contrary, I felt accepted and safe whenever I was with him.

The devil had and continued to lie to me from the very beginning, and I listened. He had enticed me to believe that entering into anorexia would give me a life free of expectations, failures, and rejection. However, he never told me that it would result in a miserable existence that would almost rob me of my life.

God's ways are the truth, and my choice to follow Him lead me to find grace and freedom.

One night as I went to leave John, he asked if he could give me a kiss goodnight? I did not see this coming. Without too much thought, I agreed, but I remember as I backed out of the driveway in my car, I said aloud, "Oh no." Every idea I had of him and just being friends came crashing down. My battle with anorexia and my fight out of it exposed many feelings and fears of losing control. This situation was no different, but this time something did feel different. I knew without any doubt that God had got me this far. He had been faithful every step of the way. I had learned that He was always with me in every situation and would not let me down. As much as I wanted to control the situation, I had this unexplainable peace with letting God be God and trust him.

While we were dating, many people were very protective of me when John came onto the scene. They had loved and nurtured me from brokenness and had watched me grow into a healthy young woman. So they were not going to let some guy stroll in and undo all their hard work.

It was hard for John, but he was determined to prove that his intentions were good. So I had peace when I was with John. I trusted God would not let me down in this area.

John and I married two years after our first meeting. Our wedding day was everything and more than I could have hoped or dreamed.

I had such peace as I prepared myself on the morning of Sunday, October 13th, 2002.

It was as though I was living someone else's life.

Although that critical decision I made back in June 1998 to travel the road to recovery was not that long ago, the person I saw back then seemed nothing like the person I felt I was.

Putting on my wedding dress was certainly a moment to remember. It was undoubtedly a moment both myself and many others thought would never happen.

Those previous tormenting voices were silent. Anorexia was not invited to our wedding day.

I felt nothing more than gratefulness and a real sense of worth.

The beauty I felt was more than the amazing dress I got to step into. I felt free from anorexia and saw myself as the Lesley God had created me to be. I was stepping into another chapter. I didn't just feel wrapped in beauty, but I was now dressing beauty.

God changed me from the inside out. I was so grateful for the journey so far, the lessons I'd learned, and the precious gift I was given—a second chance at life.

The Prize

Six years after John and I married, we were blessed with our first child, Ella Rose. Our beautiful daughter was born on December 19th, 2008. She reminds us every day that miracles do happen. My chances of conceiving a child were slim due to the extreme punishment my body endured, but God knew my heart's desire.

Two years after Ella was born, we welcomed Riley James, born February 4th, 2011, and completed our little family. Our cheeky little man.

Becoming a parent has undoubtedly shaken, stirred, and shifted a lot of my preconceived ideas.

I cannot imagine what it must have felt like for my parents all those years ago as they helplessly watched on as I slowly self-destructed.

Having children of my own, particularly a girl, has raised questions regarding how I will respond and deal with body image pressures.

My journey out of anorexia highlighted my need for Jesus. Even post anorexia, my need for Him is the core of my everyday existence. Every situation in my life reminds me that I can't do life without Him.

Knowing all He is and all He has done, I know that the best gift I can give Ella and Riley is Jesus's reality.

This is the most important legacy I can pass on to them.

I also believe that the next best gift I can give them is to be the best Lesley I can be. I want them to know I am not perfect, nor will I ever be. But, I believe I owe it to myself and them to seek wholeness in my inner world daily, and this sets a path for them to walk on.

It's incredibly tough to give love to others when you can't even love who you are. But, meeting and following Jesus has shown me real love, and I have learned to love who I am and actually like who I am.

The most powerful and personal revelation God gave to me was that HE LOVED ME and called me by name—Lesley. I will never own the right to put myself down or despise who I am, as I am His creation.

It is the one message I want my children to know and walk in. The confidence they will find in knowing His love and His unconditional love for them. The amazing part about this is that it's not about what "I" can do, but who He is. I am going to make mistakes, but He will always catch me.

I believe it is my responsibility as their mum to show and display this in my own life. I owe it to them to watch the words that come out of my mouth about myself. Even when I don't feel particularly attractive or pretty, I need to reflect on God's acceptance and love for me and walk in that myself.

I have learned to make a conscious decision not to speak about my weight or my appearance negatively, as I believe that this would insult my creator and send the wrong message to Ella and Riley.

I remind them that words such as beautiful are descriptors of someone full of kindness, love, godliness, and grace whenever there is an opportunity. The world describes beauty from what is on the outside.

I believe it's healthy to acknowledge our imperfections with a light heart and remind ourselves and our children that this is not what defines us.

I enjoy keeping as healthy as possible, but I won't allow it to control me or become obsessive.

I often sit back and look at the blessing of my two beautiful, healthy children and our little family. I can only thank God for His amazing Grace, promises, and handiwork.

Today, I am happy to say that I am free from anorexia. However, it is often hard to believe that I endured those horrible years of torment and suffering.

Although I would never wish to go through this again, I am so very grateful for what I have learned and the amazing people I met along the way. But, most importantly, I met Jesus.

Nothing could ever remove the foundation of my faith. It may get shaken, but I will forever know who created me and am eternally grateful for His love, grace, and wisdom. I know beyond any doubt that Jesus has given me a brand-new life.

Out Of The Mouth Of Babes

I remember when my daughter started kindergarten.

Being our firstborn, its fair to say I was what some would refer to as a "helicopter parent."

I wanted nothing but the best for her, and I was very aware of all the ups and downs that lay ahead for her.

She came home one day and told both myself and her dad that some of the girls at school were mean to her and when she asked them if she could play with them, they said no!

My heart broke for her.

I wanted to fix it and make everything okay for her.

My husband then said to her, "Ella, you are a beautiful, kind girl. Anyone that is your friend is a lucky person, but those that choose not to get to know you, well, that's their loss."

The next day as Ella headed to school, I wanted so much to go with her, protect her, promote her and tell everyone to be kind to her, but I couldn't!

It was a long day as I waited for her to come home.

When she was home, her dad and I asked her how her day was and whether the day was better with the other girls?

Ella replied, "The girls still didn't let me play with them, but that's okay. I just walked away and thought, "oh well, they're lost."

Although she had mixed up a word to this statement, it was powerful.

If only this were the confidence we carried through into our adult life.

Confidence in the knowledge of who we are. What we are worth.

Psalms 139:14

I praise you because I am fearfully and wonderfully made. Your works are wonderful. I know that full well.

Summary

The key to my recovery was, without any doubt, JESUS.

He was the answer and is still the answer.

Jer 29, 11-14:

For I know, the plans I have for you declares the Lord, plans to prosper you and not to harm you, plans to give you hope and a future. Then you will call upon me and come and pray to me, and I will listen to you. You will seek me and find me when you seek me with all your heart.

I am so grateful that Jesus rescued me. I was no Bible scholar. To be honest, before the commencement of the program, I rarely read my Bible at all. All that I needed was to say, 'God help me.'

He heard that simple prayer, and I opened the door and let him in to help, although I was reluctant at first!

Although I didn't want to do the things that would lead me to recovery, my heart was willing, and that was all God needed.

Jesus made me, and He knew what I needed. He knew the plan He had for me. He was just waiting for me to say, 'Yes.'

I don't believe that this specific program is necessarily the answer for every person struggling with anorexia. Still, the one thing I am sure about is that Jesus is everyone's answer. He has a specific plan for every person and is just waiting for them to say, 'Yes.'

I am forever grateful that God placed an idea in the heart of one person to assist my recovery. I had thirty-five volunteers coming to sit with me day after day, a dietician in the church who would write up a specific eating plan. So many people prepared to assist my recovery, although my recovery from anorexia appeared impossible.

God's word doesn't change, and I believe it is the basis for any recovery. God doesn't make us all the same, and He certainly doesn't make any mistakes when He creates each one of us.

Everything God showed me and spoke to me was always backed up by His word (Bible).

God has a perfect and specific plan for each person.

God started with the basics of what I believe is right for every one of us.

I LOVE YOU.

Psalm 139, 13-16 For you created my inmost being; you knit me together in my mother's womb. I praise you because I am fearfully and wonderfully made; your works are wonderful. I know that full well. My frame was not hidden from you when I was made in the secret place. When I was woven together in the depths of the earth, your eyes saw my unformed body. All the days ordained for me were written in your book before one of them came to be.

YOU ARE LESLEY.

Jeremiah 1, 4-5 The word of the Lord came to me, saying before I formed you in the womb, I knew you before you were born, I set you apart, I appointed you as a prophet to the nations.

FORGIVENESS.

Ephesians 4:32 Be kind and compassionate to one another, forgiving each other, just as Christ God forgave you.

WE ARE FLESH AND SPIRIT.

Romans 7:14-16 We know that the law is spiritual, but I am unspiritual, sold as a slave to sin. I do not understand what I do. For what I want to do, I do not do, but what I hate I do. Ephesians 6:12 For our struggle is not against flesh and blood, but against the rulers, against the authorities, against the powers of this dark world and against the spiritual forces of evil in the heavenly realms.

Ephesians 4:6 And the peace that surpasses all understanding will guard your hearts and minds in Christ Jesus.

SERVING ONLY ONE MASTER.

Matthew 6:24 No one can serve two masters. Either he will hate the one and love the other, or he will be devoted to the one and despise the other. You cannot serve both God and money.

Exodus 20:4 You shall not make for yourself an image in the form of anything in heaven above or on the earth beneath or in the waters below. You shall not bow down to them, for I, the Lord, am a jealous God, punishing the children for the sin of the fathers to the third and fourth generation of those who hate me, but showing love to a thousand generations of those who love me and keep my commandment.

James 4:8 Come near to God and he will come near to you.

MIND YOUR OWN BUSINESS.

Matthew 7:3 Why do you look at the speck of sawdust in your brother's eye but pay no attention to the plank in your own eye.

John 21:15-23 When they had finished eating, Jesus said to Simon Peter, Simon son of John, do you truly love me more than these? Yes, Lord, he said, you know that I love you. Jesus said, feed my lambs. Again, Jesus said, Simon son of John, do you truly love me? He answered, yes, Lord, you know that I love you. Jesus said, take care of my sheep. The third time He said to him, Simon son of John, do you love me? Peter was hurt because Jesus asked him the third time. Do you love me? He said Lord, you know all things; you know that I love you. Jesus said, feed my sheep. I tell you the truth, when you were younger you dressed yourself and went where you wanted, but when you are old you will stretch out your hands and someone else will dress you and lead you where you do not want to go. Jesus said this is to indicate the kind of death by which Peter would glorify God. Then he said to him, follow me.

Peter turned up and saw that the disciple whom Jesus loved was following them. This was the one who had leaned back against Jesus at the supper and had said, Lord, who is going to betray you? When Peter saw him, he asked, "Lord, what about him?" Jesus answered, "If I want him to remain alive until I return, what is that to you? you must follow me"

Hebrews 12:4 In your struggle against sin, you have not yet resisted to the point of shedding your blood. And you have forgotten that word of encouragement that addresses you as sons: my son, do not make light of the Lords discipline, and do not lose heart when he rebukes you, because the Lord disciplines those He loves, and He punishes everyone He accepts as a son.

Nehemiah 8:10 The joy of the Lord is your strength.

THE BLOOD OF JESUS.

John 3:16 For God so loved the world, that he gave his one and only son.

RESIST THE DEVIL, AND HE WILL FLEE.

James 4:7, Therefore, submit to God. Resist the devil, and he will flee from you.

What I have come to understand personally and what excites me, is that Jesus is interested in each of us.

Whenever I am struggling with a situation in my life, Jesus will reveal something in me that needs to change. Although we tend to look outward and see the faults in others and what we think they have to change, Jesus sees an opportunity for us to grow. We cannot control others, but we can control our thoughts and reactions. Creating an opportunity for positive change in our own lives.

John's Message

March 28th, 1999, I left my home in New Zealand with the hope of a working holiday and fresh adventures.

I headed off with a three-year plan of traveling and working throughout Australia. My first stop was Port-Douglas in Far North Queensland, where I worked for three months. I had a cousin living in Perth, WA, so I thought that would be my next stop until I could save enough to take on Europe.

I found work quickly in Perth and felt it was time to establish myself in a local church after some time.

I started attending the "Christian Outreach Centre" in East Perth. I hadn't been attending the church long when the church pastor announced that a film crew would be visiting the following Sunday to film a church member and her recovery from anorexia.

After the film crew had been at church, I was intrigued to watch this television documentary on this cute blonde that I had so often seen singing in the church choir every Sunday morning.

I watched a movie at a local cinema the night the documentary was to be aired. Unfortunately, the movie would not finish in time for me to return home, so I decided to leave the film and head back to watch a "real" story!

I left the movie early and raced home to watch this documentary that so many talked about at the church.

I can only describe watching the documentary as a God moment. As I watched her story, I could think of nothing other than how courageous she was. I could see a special person and someone I would be honoured to know.

I now had to work out how to build up the courage to talk to her and possibly ask her out.

I was new to the church and a little intimidated by this petite, good-looking blonde movie star!

I needed to develop a good plan, and as Jesus was my wingman, I knew I could do it!

I had to think about the conversation I would initiate with her carefully.

It took me four weeks to pluck up the courage to eventually talk to this girl. I had heard she was a dental nurse, and as I hadn't seen a dentist for some time, I figured this would be the perfect conversation starter.

Being in the spotlight at church, she always had a steady stream of people queuing to talk to her after the church service. I was lingering close by, waiting for my opportunity.

I was nervous but played the innocent Kiwi backpacker to my advantage. As soon as I had her attention, I quickly asked her if she had a business card as I was eager to visit a dentist.

She was friendly and polite and wrote down her work contact details. Then, as it was veering close to lunchtime, I knew I had only a few seconds to suggest Plan B of my strategic goal—a lunch date!

I told her I was new to Perth and would like to buy her lunch and to suggest anywhere to eat. So we headed out to a casual Thai eatery in Victoria Park.

We must have been there for around four hours. The conversation flowed with ease.

Lesley was funny with a dry sense of humour. The girl that sat in front of me contrasted the picture of the anorexic girl I saw on the TV documentary. She seemed free and appeared to carry no wounds.

I remember looking across the table and thinking, "this is the girl I will marry."

I had come from my journey through depression, so there was an instant connection. I looked at this girl that at one stage, was so unwell that the medical profession had given her only days to survive. I knew that she was a living miracle.

She had a wholeness about her, and yet she seemed so free for someone who had been so sick and bound up. I saw God in and all around her life as we spoke, which attracted me to Lesley.

We dated for two years and were married in October 2002. Our wedding day was surreal. The church was a big part of our life, so we decided to say our vows during the Sunday morning service so that all of our friends and family could be there to celebrate with us.

I had my brother as my best man beside me, our arms raised, praising God. I felt such peace and knew that I was marrying God's choice for my life.

We now have two beautiful, happy, and healthy children. Lesley has a normal relationship with food. Even when I first met Lesley, I never viewed her as a recovered anorexic nor treated her like one. Both Lesley and myself are real foodies and love going out and entertaining with food.

When God heals, He leaves no stone unturned, and we go through the fire and come out the other side, not smelling of any smoke.

That certainly was how I saw Lesley. So I'm mindful that some people reading this book will not see a way out or maybe no future.

There is a God in heaven with the best plan for your life and wants to see you set free. He wants to expose the lie that you may have believed about yourself. Unfortunately, Lesley could not overcome anorexia in her strength, will, or power.

He will help and heal you if you trust Him, just as he did for my wife.

A Final Word From Sandra: *It seemed to be a blessed mix of people of different strengths involved in this rescue mission.*

We had the professionals in the psychologist and the GP, we then had Sascha, me, and all the volunteers who were amateurs at helping those with anorexia, but God took our "willing to help" hearts and made it work.

There was also an army of people praying earnestly for Lesley, including her family, my family, others in the church, friends, etc.

Certainly, it might not have been a scientifically proven approach for treating anorexia. Still, its power was in the spiritual healing, renewing her mind, and I believe the consistent love shown by all involved. As they faithfully turned up day after day, she was reminded that although they had busy lives of their own, they chose to give their time to her. The only conclusion Lesley could make was that these people must genuinely care for her. She was of great value and worth helping. It was a vast support network, all for her. This love, I believe, seeped into her heart over time and significantly strengthened her.

The proof that Lesley is free from anorexia is that years later, she is still a normal, healthy weight and not bothered by those things that once troubled her. She is also not depressed but a very happy and fulfilled person and is a delight to be around.

She loves God and loves life.

Set free indeed.

Thank You

Mum and Dad, Fiona, Robyn, Sue, Vicky, Barbara and Lynn for never giving up. Sandra, Sascha, and Bruce I am forever grateful.

To all the volunteers
My real-life angels:

Trudy	Liz	Michelle
Margaret	Bernardine	Lyn
Vanda	Clare	Caroline
Lynette	Cathy	Ron
Sue	Carol	Tracy
Helen	Allison	Ps. Geoff & Rhonda
Claire	Henrikke	

I couldn't have done it without you all.

Finally, to my supportive husband John, daughter Ella and son Riley, Thankyou.

www.ingramcontent.com/pod-product-compliance
Lightning Source LLC
Chambersburg PA
CBHW051456290426
44109CB00016B/1778